# CYBERTALK *that* SELLS

Herschell Gordon Lewis and Jamie Murphy

D1243310

CONTEMPORARY BOOKS

**Library of Congress Cataloging-in-Publication Data**

Lewis, Herschell Gordon
    Cybertalk that sells : the ultimate source of words, phrases,
banners, and buzzwords for selling your products, services, and
ideas through the new digital and interactive media / Herschell
Gordon Lewis and Jamie Murphy.
         p.    cm.
    ISBN 0-8092-2923-4
     1. Internet advertising.   2. Advertising copy.   3. Internet
marketing.   4. Internet (Computer network)   I. Murphy, Jamie.
II. Title.
HF6146.I58L48    1998
659.13—dc21                         97-50104
                                               CIP

Interior design and production by Susan H. Hartman

Published by Contemporary Books
A division of NTC/Contemporary Publishing Group, Inc.
4255 West Touhy Avenue, Lincolnwood (Chicago), Illinois 60646-1975 U.S.A.
Copyright © 1998 by Herschell Gordon Lewis and Jamie Murphy
All rights reserved. No part of this book may be reproduced, stored in a retrieval
system, or transmitted in any form or by any means, electronic, mechanical,
photocopying, recording, or otherwise, without the prior permission of
NTC/Contemporary Publishing Group, Inc.
Printed in the United States of America
International Standard Book Number: 0-8092-2923-4
18   17   16   15   14   13   12   11   10   9   8   7   6   5   4   3   2   1

# Contents

# Acknowledgments

ALL authors of books dedicated to interactive commerce owe a debt of gratitude to Tim Berners-Lee, who "founded" the Internet. We thank him for his foresight—his child has grown into a giant.

Tribute is due as well to Mark Andreessen, the originator of the leading Web browser Netscape; and yes, to Bill Gates, whose ubiquitous competition forces innovations throughout the electronic universe.

On a personal level, Herschell Gordon Lewis thanks his son Robert Lewis, coauthor of *Selling on the Net*, who is an inexhaustible wellspring of usable information; and his brilliant spouse, Margo Lewis, whose patience and inspiration are both remarkable and boundless.

Jamie Murphy would like to thank his lovely wife, Debbie, for her encouragement; his children, Casie and Jamie, for letting him work in peace; his parents, Joan and Brannen, for their continued support; Dr. Charles Hofacker for his cyberguidance; and Dr. Edward Wotring, for his counsel.

Both authors are indebted to Richard Hagle, the indefatigable editor at NTC Business Books, for gently pushing and shoving until the manuscript was delivered.

Our thanks to them. And our thanks to *you*, who have given us the ultimate compliment by seeing enough value in this book to buy it. May it be worthwhile for us all!

# Preface

WHAT the &^$%#@* are you guys writing about?

Selling through e-mail is the newest, most fascinating, and most challenging marketing procedure human beings have devised. Unfortunately, it's also the most frustrating and most misunderstood marketing procedure, populated by countless know-it-alls, know-nothings, and would-bes.

Tens of millions of advertisers have launched messages on the World Wide Web; most have been disappointed in the results, and yes, some have been pleased. But as of this writing, few major marketers have dipped a toe in the calmer, far less expensive waters of e-mail. Lots of books on Internet advertising are out there. (In fact, we've written some of them.) Many of those books lay out rules for advertising on the Web—and not all those rules are in agreement. Here we tackle a new challenge: Selling by e-mail.

E-mail has gigantic advantages over standard website marketing. Budget is only one of those advantages; the capability of quick revisions is another. The combination of these two advantages makes testing one approach against another both feasible and logical, a third plus of e-mail marketing.

You'd think these three advantages would bring marketers flocking to the e-mail shores.

Nope.

Not yet.

You'd think the simplicity of the medium would bring hypereffective messages to e-mail.

Nope.

Seldom.

Here we have a medium with hundreds of millions of potential customers all over the globe, and advertisers are still running . . . well, they're running *advertising*. So much of that advertising is wrong for this medium that they're wasting hundreds of millions of dollars every day.

Maybe, just maybe, we can be of some help. This is a short book, so it's easy to read and absorb. It's a focused book, so the information doesn't wander off into arcane areas where it isn't pertinent. And it's a hard-boiled book, so despite the necessary injection of background and theory (just to be sure we're following the same radar signal), you can use it immediately instead of leaving it to gather dust on a bookshelf.

We enjoyed putting this book together, because we believe the subject hasn't been sliced and diced yet. If we're in luck, you'll enjoy it too.

# 1

# A Whole New Medium

## We're Not in Kansas Anymore (We're Everywhere!)

### Birth of the Network of Networks

Who hasn't heard of the Internet? More to the point, who hasn't

- established a website?
- surfed the Internet and its commercial child the World Wide Web?

1

- had a negative, dampening experience either within a proprietary website or while visiting websites?
- all of the above?

Where did it all come from? How could this monster have sprung up in our midst without our knowing it?

In the mid 1960s the Cold War was red hot. Still smarting from the Soviet Union's early lead in the space race, the United States was throwing money at scientific projects. Anything electronic seemed to be a logical target. After all, didn't the U.S. control the output of computer chips, software, and that yet-to-be-born speck on the horizon, personal computers?

In 1966, Bob Taylor, a psychoacoustician (yes, such a professional title does exist) and director of the computer research program at the U.S. Department of Defense's Advanced Research Projects Agency (ARPA) suggested to his boss, Charlie Herzfeld, the possibility of linking various research center computers via a common interface. The common interface would allow different computers, regardless of the make or brand, to talk to each other.

After a 20-minute off-the-cuff meeting, Herzfeld plopped another $1 million into Taylor's budget to develop and build a small experimental network. Thus the concept of networking was born in an electronic manger, with wise men as both witnesses and shepherds.

Three years later, on Labor Day weekend 1969—still before the first personal computer had been assembled, except for laboratory demonstrations—Taylor's project became a reality. A computer in Los Angeles connected and conversed with a computer in Menlo Park, California. Soon a computer in Santa Barbara and another at the University of Utah joined the network. The Internet, then called the ARPAnet, was born with little fanfare and no commercial intentions or expectations.

Slowly but surely, Department of Defense installations and universities joined the ever-expanding network. These organizations plugged their computer networks into the Internet—the network of networks.

Move ahead, to 1997: Some 20 million computers, or *hosts*, already were connected to the Internet. Because many of these hosts represent a network of computers, the total number of computers connected to the Internet extended far beyond 20 million. That was 1997. Of all communication media, none has mushroomed—no, *skyrocketed*—at the incredible speed the Internet has achieved. And it keeps on growing.

## A Whole New Culture

Even if the Internet weren't growing faster than a science-fiction creature, doubling in size as we look at it, estimating the number of Internet users would be difficult to say the least. There is no central Internet authority. And the Internet is global, not just a United States playground. In fact, almost every Internet "expert" (and they abound by the hundreds) predicts that the fastest percentile growth in number of users during the first decade of the twenty-first century will be in countries other than the United States.

Originally, the Internet was like a private club—a tightly controlled members-only community of scientists and academicians. Even in the early 1990s, one had to be a hard-core computer geek, with modem in hand, to use the Internet. Although there were no restrictions on who could access the Internet, users had to know the technology.

Today, access to most sites is open to anyone. From kindergarten to college, students often have free Internet access through their schools. Individuals also connect to the Internet at work in businesses or government organizations. Companies like America Online, which weren't even a gleam in anyone's eye in the 1970s, are now spending hundreds of millions of dollars to entice people onto the Internet and establishing a multitude of ancillary attractions to keep the electronic proletariat interested.

A mid-1997 estimate put the number of American Internet users at around 50 million. This is roughly double the number of Internet users of the previous year (and may be suspect, as only 30 million American homes had a computer, let alone a modem). Still, most forecasts continue to predict similar growth patterns. And today's Internet users are a marketer's demographic dream, if perhaps a scientist's nightmare—with above-average income and education, curiosity, and short attention spans, to which the Internet seems to cater.

Not only do today's Internet users share common demographics, they also share a community. Call them net heads, cyberati, digerati, or netizens—no matter what the name, a special culture exists on the Internet. Just as a marketer would research a foreign country before doing business there, the same principle holds true when analyzing the marketing potential of the Internet. The professional marketer's first assignment is to know the culture of the target group.

The Internet began as an isolated community of hard-core scientists cryptically communicating among themselves for decades. Slowly but surely, common values and norms and etiquette peculiar to the Net (*netiquette*) evolved in this restricted space. And although nerds and scientists no longer represent the majority of Internet users, the community values they defined still govern the Internet.

## A Whole New Medium

Remember Vice President Al Gore's 1996 campaign metaphor, the information superhighway? While not technically referring to the Internet, Gore did introduce the Internet to much of mainstream America. Like a highway, the Internet has several lanes, each reserved for a special type of Internet driving. (The two most popular lanes, e-mail and the World Wide Web, are explained in Chapters 2 and 3.)

This is one highway that keeps getting faster and wider. And like too many highways, the traffic consistently exceeds the highway's physical expansion. An avalanche of emerging technologies guarantees that construction to increase the speed limits and lanes on the information superhighway is far from finished—and may never be, like an airport that forever is adding terminals and landing strips as traffic demands expansion. The small black-and-white 1950s television with two or three channels bears little resemblance to today's big-screen digital HDTV with stereo speakers and hundreds of channels. And so it will be with the Internet.

What a challenge: Expand with technology or be left in the dust. The casual surfer invariably loses pace.

*Rule 1: Speak to the individual, not to a group.*

A number of pundits and prognosticators agree that one by one, the Internet will encompass the telephone, fax, television, movies, radio, and most print communication. However, as a commercial medium, the Internet (or more correctly, the World Wide Web) is not and cannot be a true mass medium. Rather, it is a gigantic conglomeration of niche media. And how do niche media differ from mass media? In dedication to communication with the *individual*. The Web is (or should be, if the marketer approaches it properly) a one-to-one selling instrument.

## The Rocky Road to a Multimedia Extravaganza

Cynics have a term for new software packages developers hype (promote) in trade and consumer media as breakthrough technological advances: *vaporware*. This hyped software, if it ever does come to market, usually fails woefully to work as promised. Too much Internet software has been vaporous. It's natural that this makes the marketing targets edgy and skeptical.

Even Internet software that works as promised still depends upon a fast Internet connection. In the antediluvian 1980s, when modems transmitted data at 300 bytes per second (commonly referred to as *baud*), users were patient. They had to be. But then came 600 baud; 1,200; 2,400; 9,600. Today, modems slower than 33,600 baud are considered archaic. The majority of modem-equipped computers manufactured at this writing include a 57,600 baud modem (commonly referred to as a 56K modem). Newer technologies such as ISDN promise to make 56K baud seem like life in the slow lane.

Phone companies now offer ISDN connections at more than 100,000 baud and have announced ASDL technology at over 1 million baud. Cable television operators roll out cable modems with speeds exceeding 1 million baud. Wireless connections via satellites also promise speeds above 1 million baud. And these are just the technologies that we know of at the time of this writing. Clearly, Internet access speeds will get faster.

All the access speed in the world, though, is of little value if the Internet's backbones are clogged. Backbones are the Internet's pipelines, but the pipes can pipe only so much data. Major backbone providers are constantly upgrading their capacity to keep up with demand.

Today, the fattest backbones transmit data at a mind-boggling 600 million baud. But to get to these superfast backbones, the data has to work its way up a series of ever-larger conduits, starting with your modem.

But look out! Each step along the way, more users jump in. If the pipes are clogged or overworked, the data transmission slows down and can even come to a virtual stop. Minor brownouts are common from 9:00 A.M. to 5:00 P.M. on weekdays. European users try to cram their Internet access into early hours, claiming that they wait forever when the bulk of U.S. users come online. America Online's entire system was down for more than a day in 1996, and the system's inability to cope with expansion has been a source of sour humor. ("What's the difference between America Online and a computer virus? A computer virus works.") Unfair as the criticisms may be, because America Online (AOL) actually is a miracle of efficiency, those criticisms represent the twenty-first century attitude toward the Internet and the World Wide Web: I want it. I want it now. No excuses.

But be of good cheer!

Don't let these embryonic hiccups discourage you. An early version of color television was a thin, colored plastic sheet stuck on the face of a black-and-white television screen. Just bear in mind that more changes loom ahead on the Internet frontier. Few of those affect Rule 1: *Speak to the individual, not to a group.*

## A Powerful Double-Edged Sword

How much would you spend to broadcast your ignorance and stupidity or to alienate customers? Hordes of businesses and individuals are using the Internet to do just that. Most articles and books hyping the Internet fail to emphasize that it is a deadly double-edged sword that can slice open the wielder as well as the target.

Early webmasters—those doughty individuals charged with the responsibility of setting up sites—too often thought in terms of "flash" and acquisition of a personal sample for themselves instead of what the average Web surfer might want to see. In other words, ego reigned over business sense. Sites reflected what the originator wanted to show (logos and individual executive biographies) instead of what the surfer wanted to explore (deals and excitement). Rates for setting up sites were all over the lot. (They still are, and probably always will be.) As a result, too many sites expected too much. They disappeared quietly, unmourned by all except those who had spent money creating them.

In traditional media, a poorly executed advertising campaign or promotion is akin to shooting yourself in the foot. On the World Wide Web, a mistake may blow off your leg. The disgusted surfer may never, never again darken your website.

*Rule 2: Keep the download fast.*

*Rule 3: Keep the message simple.*

*Rule 4: Be ready to respond quickly.*

Remember the fairy tale *The Emperor's New Clothes*? The emperor was convinced he was wearing a fine outfit but just couldn't see it. No one else could see it either . . . because it didn't exist. The emperor paid a great sum to look stupid. Businesses and individuals are putting a Web spin on this classic fable, investing in websites and massive e-mails that broadcast ignorance and alienate potential customers.

*The purpose of this book is to prevent YOU from buying the emperor's clothes on your own planned or existing website.*

Volvo had one of the first automobile websites. Unfortunately, Volvo failed to understand a critical aspect of Internet culture: e-mail is a handy tool for quickly venting frustrations, which Volvo owners did. Faced with a flood of negative e-mails and insufficient staff, Volvo shut down the website's e-mail option. This solved Volvo's immediate problem; but even as it accomplished this questionable success, it emasculated Volvo's website. The Web's competitive advantage over other media, interactivity, evaporates without e-mail.

Even worse, Volvo missed the opportunity to develop a one-to-one relationship with a select clientele. These special cybercustomers took the time to visit the website, knocking on Volvo's virtual front door.

An amusing *Wall Street Journal* article chronicled responses to e-mails sent to two dozen major corporate websites. These short messages asked for further product or sales information. Overall, the queried corporations failed miserably. One of every three sites never responded at all, and only three sites adequately answered a simple question. Two sites took a sluggish three weeks to respond, in a medium where users measure response time in hours . . . no, make that minutes.

The Internet is the most powerful medium yet invented. Take heed though: The power cuts both ways. Throughout this book, you will discover how to harness the Internet's awesome power safely and profitably. Doses of Internet reality therapy will protect you from this powerful medium's devastating negative potential.

Ready? Let's roll!

# 2

# E-mail

## The Most Significant Advance Since Sliced Bread?

### What It Is

Just as word processors made correction fluid a relic, e-mail has the ingredients that, if used to full potential, could turn the dedicated fax machine into the last twentieth-century antique.

E-mail makes sense to everybody. For bean counters, e-mail is faster, cheaper, and easier than the fax. For hedonists, e-mailing is more fun than faxing, and considerably more private. For interactive professionals, e-mail is a powerful new arrow in their communicative quiver.

A fax's output is limited to ink and paper. E-mail is more. E-mail walks, talks, and some might even say it thinks. Audio files, video files, even computer programs soar through cyberspace attached to an e-mail's wings.

Even with messages destined for ink and paper, e-mail reigns supreme over the fax. The fax sends a picture of a document. E-mail sends the digits; the document is ready for word processing, filing, or printing. Word processing a fax is a time-consuming, no-win choice between retyping the document or an electronic mélange of optical scanning, editing, and file manipulation, each of which is labor intensive and equipment heavy.

## What Works Best for This? Or This? Or That?

E-mail actually is supercompetitive with traditional communication methods, its reach and effectiveness limited only by the connectivity between parties. Electronic communication, even in its early years, is acknowledged as the next generation of message transmission.

As more people use e-mail, its power surges exponentially. Internet luminary and ethernet inventor Bob Metcalfe offers this formula as a means of measuring a network's value: the square of its number of users. It's hard to argue with Metcalfe's "law." Consider this obvious truism: Having the only telephone in the world would be of no value, but the value increases with each new telephone it can call.

And legions more "e-literates" plug in every day. As online communication becomes easier and more global, advertisers rent banner space on websites to support this user friendly, 24-hour service.

As many of the early experimenters with online advertising have discovered to their chagrin, the cyberspace advertising medium is not the be-all, end-all its fanatical advocates claim. It's best to focus on exploiting the competitive advantage cyberspace has over preexisting media. And two unique advantages—novelty, and control over the seller/buyer relationship—may be more emotional than real.

## Electronic Communities

Cyberspace communities, sprouting and thriving thanks to e-mail, are classic examples of Metcalfe's equation. These global enclaves cover a multitude of subjects in an ongoing, westerly-traveling dialogue. Via e-mail, like-minded cyberenthusiasts from Australia to Zimbabwe discuss such diverse and specialized topics as miniature desert rose gardening, South African rugby, and Tour de France cycling.

Each digital community creates its own culture, its own protocol, and its own substance. Pick a topic and more than likely a *listserv* or *usenet* covers it or something similar. Listservs and usenets, while technically different, serve the same purpose. Both permit anyone with an e-mail capability to join an electronic discussion group. Any group member can *post* (jargon for sending an e-mail message, or for the message itself) to every other group member.

Groups range from a handful of members to thousands. Volume, or the amount of daily e-mails posted, easily can total tens of thousands. Yes, if you join an active listserv or usenet it could mean receiving thousands of e-mails daily! Some listserv and usenet junkies join hundreds of these digital communities.

Thanks to the Internet's inherent freedom and global reach, this diverse collection of communities more closely resembles Star Trek's Federation of Planets than the United Nations. As the famous line from *Forrest Gump* might be adapted, e-mail is like a box of chocolates—you never know what you're going to get.

Savvy travelers study a country's history, geography, commerce, and culture long before setting foot on foreign soil. The informed traveler thinks through problems such as currency, visas, and exchange rates ahead of time. The itinerary profits from visits to historic monuments, natural wonders, and special interest destinations. Familiarity with the country's history and culture yields a broader view and deeper impression of the country's natives.

While globetrotters can face life-threatening situations—civil war, mugging, bombing, carjacking—cyberspace travelers face different perils. E-mail pitfalls are usually financial, emotional, or both.

## What It Can Be

Yes, e-mail is a powerful communication tool bursting with untapped potential. But this power carries a price and a responsibility. Slipshod e-mailing broadcasts ignorance. The broadcast's reach and damage vary depending on the mistake.

Typographical errors are relatively harmless—note that word *relatively*—and often ignored. In the Internet's pioneering days, limited access and complicated e-mail software for word processing made proofreading a rare option. The most common excuse for misspellings was and is that many e-mail programs don't have a spell-checker. Some users prefer a less formal, abbreviated style with little or no capitalization (e.e. cummings would be right at home in some users' circles). In the pioneering days, capitalization was out. But the pioneering days are past, and an absolute rule of communication is that you can't go wrong by using proper grammar and punctuation.

A more painful e-mail mistake is sending a targeted message to the wrong person. This happens often. Ouch! Chapter 5 of this book will put you ahead of the game on effectively addressing and organizing your e-mail missives.

E-mail's pinnacle of stupidity—electronic junk mail, usually commercial, called *spam*—has the unique potential of reaching and ticking off millions of people in an instant. Computerized *e-bots* (electronic robots) cull the Internet for e-mail addresses—and once electronic junk-mailers grab a name, they rarely let go. Spammers buy and sell e-mail lists among themselves, so lists become larger, more prevalent, and inevitably cheaper.

High-speed servers then spew the same message to the millions of e-mail addresses nabbed by e-bots or bought on the open market. As of this writing, costs range from $200 to $2,000 for randomly impressing or angering 1 million people almost instantaneously. Deluxe spamming software includes options such as less work for the sender, targeted e-mail lists, and even anonymity.

Oh, yes. Spamming is so detested that spammers use aliases and fake names, sometimes even other Internet service providers' servers, to conceal their identity. A great way to do business, eh? Launch the spam, then hide. (Actually, we're being both wry and severe, because the only logical way to keep score of the effectiveness of an e-mail message is by response . . . and the recipient has to respond to a specific online address. So tracking the message source isn't all that difficult. And individuals always have the option of cutting off unanticipated e-mail.)

So, like its canned namesake, spam represents benefit or curse, depending on the recipient's personality and state of mind when the message comes in. Some welcome a message, viewing it as recognition of their existence; others resent the intrusion.

An undeniable benefit of this type of communication is that it generally forces us to stay abreast of marketing trends. Spammers (and Web marketers in general) live on their wits. If they're to stay in business longer than one week, they aren't about to transmit stupid, nonspecific, useless messages.

# E-mail Basics

With some guidelines and forethought, you can minimize embarrassment and maximize e-mail's potential. Although e-mail and snail mail both require common sense, the e-mail community has its own special culture complete with customs, traditions, and taboos. Following a few simple guidelines will make e-mail easier and more enjoyable for both parties, more profitable for the sender, and less harmful to the concept of e-mail marketing.

### Look Before You Leap, Think Before You Send

E-mail's phenomenal simplicity advantage over snail mail too often launches lightning-fast but emotionally charged digital missiles. Sending a letter necessitates a sequence of steps, with time for reflection built into each step.

Snail mail's requisite materials—paper, pen or word processor, envelope, and stamps—stifle many a thought. And something started does not mean something sent. Often the traditional writing process offers opportunity for reflection and refinement. The final version, if ever sent, is tamer and more prosaic than the impulsive first draft.

E-mail is really too easy. Firing off e-mail to one recipient or to a million is as simple as a couple of mouse clicks. All too often, passion rules. Proofing, reflection, purpose, attitude, and a bevy of other considerations fall by the wayside, victims of e-mail's simplicity.

Worse, every e-mail may be a matter of public record. If you dispatch a message to an active group, thousands of users have a copy of something you might well regret having sent. We already have witnessed case after case in which a sender loses a job or a lawsuit because of an unwise e-mail transmission.

This isn't a book about legal issues, or, for that matter, about master strategies. But a mild touch on this touchy subject: Have a plan. Have a purpose. Have a strategy in mind. Don't fire until your rhetorical cannon is loaded and aimed.

From the viewpoint of both logic and psychology, e-mail isn't different from snail mail. Look before you leap and think before you send.

## Who Invited You?

A person's e-mail account is private territory. Who gave you permission to use their e-mail address, send them e-mail, and take up disk space on their e-mail account?

Every e-mail received must be processed. The recipient can delete the e-mail, never bothering to read it; read it and delete it; or read it and respond. And each e-mail either clutters up the receiver's inbox, is filed for future attention, or has to be deleted. No matter who gets your e-mail, from a close friend to a total stranger, you are sending them work, taking their time.

Yes, of course, use e-mail to contact prospective clients or collaborators. But keep in mind the intrusive, often disliked aspect of unsolicited e-mail. You had better have a darned good explanation for invading a receiver's cyberturf. Chapter 7 of this book walks you through a few winning e-mail formats.

## Mind Your Manners

In conjunction with politely knocking on someone's e-mail door, traditional manners are important. E-mail's ease of use is no excuse for forgetting to say "please" and "thank you."

Sharp marketers profit from e-mail's simplicity to keep the communication going. Quickly acknowledging receipt of an e-mail takes an instant, and tells the sender: *You matter*. And how does the mailer, especially the commercial mailer, convince the recipient to send an acknowledgment? That's part of what this book is about. The very timeliness of the medium helps tie it to great motivators such as fear, guilt, and exclusivity. So an e-mail that attacks the recipient's fears, hopes, greed, or need for status is hard to ignore.

## Keep It Neat

One of e-mail's greatest tricks is the "reply" command, which makes responding to incoming e-mail a click away. The reply usually contains the body of the original e-mail. While this makes replying fast and easy, it also creates some long and ugly e-mails. And it brands the sender as either a *newbie* or a *bandwidth hog*. Neat, precise e-mails are a noble goal; but only experience (and by experience we mean *responses*) will let you know if they work best for any specific publicizing, self-aggrandizing, proselytizing, or merchandising project. (Some examples of e-mail messages, ranging from lame to powerful, are reproduced in Chapter 7.)

Human indolence is a mighty weapon for any marketer. The less work your target has to do in order to respond, the more likely it is that you'll get a response.

Most e-mail software uses increasing layers of the > symbol to keep track of reply messages within an e-mail stack. This helps identify who is speaking, similar to quoting someone. For example:

The current e-mail contains no symbols.

>The previous e-mail contains one symbol.

>>The e-mail previous to that contains two symbols.

>>>And so forth.

>>>>Until the multitude of replies

>>>>>evolve into a gobbledygook

>>>>>>of confusing

>>>>>>>and hard-to-read

>>>>>>>>symbols.

In addition to making messages increasingly difficult to follow, continually including the previous message makes each response larger in its number of characters. In some circles, this is a waste of precious band-width—the longer the message, the more bandwidth used to send it.

The jury is still out on how much original e-mail to include in a response. Some prefer starting anew, as if with a letter or fax. Others prefer deleting irrelevant passages, responding directly underneath the remaining text. Rarely, if ever, should the original e-mail be re-sent in its entirety. When pondering how much quoted text to include, remember: If in doubt, cut it out.

### Testing the Waters: Lurking

Internet travel guides are cropping up in bookstores and libraries. And, like weeds, they expand and die quickly. The obsolescence factor in any type of computer-related text (with the possible exception of this one) is obscenely quick. These cyberspace maps review websites, listservs, and usenets. Guidebooks help, but the only way to experience and profit from a listserv or usenet is to test the waters and join the community.

(Note, please: These descriptions are of cyberspace communities, not of sites on the World Wide Web. In the interest of completeness, we're now discussing groups and chatrooms. Not to worry. Much more on the commercial aspects of e-mail is coming up.)

The obligatory first step in exploring any e-mail community is to read the FAQ, short for "frequently asked questions." This question/answer list addresses common questions, establishing each commune's protocol, culture, and esprit de corps.

For example, in a typical moderated group, a moderator culls out inappropriate posts, yielding fewer, blander, yet consistently on-topic posts. On-topic, of course, is directly tied to the moderator's interpretation.

Unmoderated groups are more active, wilder, and less focused. But the looser nature and higher volume lead to a few incisive and entertaining posts.

Like a cultural anthropologist trying to blend into a primitive society or tropical rain forest, you can remain invisible to the group at large. After reading the FAQ, the next step is to lurk in the shadows for a few weeks. Until you post, no one knows you are there.

*Lurking* means nothing more than reading each day's posts and making notes to yourself as you observe the natives. Most e-mail communities parallel radio talk shows: a small percentage of residents account for a large percentage of posts. And the lurker parallels a consistent listener, sensitive to individual voices and points of view.

Sooner rather than later, lurkers recognize community residents. A few members are worth reading every time, usually for insights or entertainment. Some members' posts are not worth reading; like traditional junk mail, these packages are thrown away unopened. Some members live to post, chiming in daily to get their electronic fix.

A few cantankerous inhabitants live to fight. These sourpusses pick on newbies and fight with old timers by sending negative messages, commonly called *flames*. A few rhetorical artists flame subtly, with a tongue-in-cheek sense of humor. Most flames, though, are instantaneous and emotional; and most flame wars degenerate into a drivel of juvenile name-calling, soiling both parties.

Reading the FAQs and lurking are the easiest ways to avoid flames and enjoy participating in an electronic community.

## Show Me More!

Chapter 5 of this book clues you in on an e-mail's subject heading and addressing scheme. Chapter 6 gives you a giant list of effective e-mail words and starter phrases. Chapter 7 lays out a compendium of rules and includes examples of e-mails that follow those rules and e-mails that ignore those rules.

Rocketing out batches of e-mail to the right targets is the kingdom of heaven for Internet marketers—if you're the emperor and the emperor is wearing clothes.

# 3

# Cyberspace
# Field of Dreams

## If You Build It,
## They Will Come.
## (Oh, Yeah?)

### Hyped-Up Hyperspace

In spite of the amazing new universe e-mail has opened to those who venture into cyberspace, the electronic postal system lacks a good public relations agent. Marketing media gush over the Internet's hyper-hyped application, the World Wide Web, and give ho-hum treatment to Internet e-mail.

Maybe that's because e-mail is so much easier to formulate and so much less expensive to propel than a website. Or maybe it's because the typical marketer is uneasy with using words instead of a blend of words and graphics to grab attention and generate response.

Even the specialized trade press dedicated to electronic communication has studiedly ignored e-mail or downplayed its advantages. The Web came online in 1994, immediately stealing the headlines.

And rightfully so. After all, e-mail sends only a bunch of words, sometimes with audio or video attachments, over the Internet. The World Wide Web shows words and pictures, even plays sound and movie clips. Simply put, the Web is more stimulating than e-mail.

## Just Plug and Play— No Experience Necessary

Describing e-mail is fairly straightforward. You use a computer to send messages via the Internet. People who can grasp the basics of what a computer or even a fax can do can also perceive e-mail's capabilities without ever seeing it perform. Sending e-mail the first time is fun, but the fun is based on novelty—the experience is pretty much what was expected. And we all know how short the life of novelty can be.

Not so the World Wide Web.

Let's take just a couple of minutes to look at the Web. The Web is the father of e-mail, just as the Internet is the father of the Web. Confused marketers sometimes lump Web advertising and e-mail marketing into a single block. The lumping has some validity; it's similar to lumping a magazine with the subscription mailings for that magazine.

Marketing on the World Wide Web has to be experienced. The experience can be delightful or painful, depending on how much you spend, how much you take in, and (too often) how highly you value just being on the Web, profitably or not.

Calling the Web an interactive medium is a truism, provided the individual marketer understands that interactivity transcends passive observation. Seeing is believing, but participation is what brings action and results.

No matter how much a man reads about childbirth, he will never participate in a conversation in which mothers discuss labor pains. Fortunately, the labor pains of becoming adept in Web marketing are available to both men and women, all types of marketers, and would-be users who want to see for themselves what it's all about before following false footsteps that lead to quagmire instead of terra firma.

Books are great; properly digested, they too qualify as interactive. Proof: You probably will use some of the tips in this one. But the only way to master the Web is to get out there and surf. You'll soon find special niches where the Web outperforms other media.

You know what else you'll find? Clutter.

Clutter is the result of too many marketers playing on the Web, like a bunch of kids playing on the beach. And your biggest competitor is clutter. It drives people away, numbs reactions, and kills response.

That's why your cybermessages have to "pop." Clutter in cyberspace is far worse than in the previous clutter champion, television. Your target individual's attention span is even shorter than that of someone watching the fifth commercial in a TV "pod."

*The three e-mail imperatives: Grab. Shake. Offer.*

## Analysis + Creative Action = A Winner

Success stems not only from your willingness to expose your intellect and abilities on websites. If you can generate analysis of your message, followed by the decision to move that analysis up to the highest plateau of creative action, you'll solidify what the individual has seen (plastic information) into what he or she can use intelligently (concrete information).

Other than in one-to-one conversation, analysis and creative action serve you better in website marketing than in any other type of force communication. This approach gives you an empirical base whose validity is tied 100 percent to your own ability to mirror the marketplace: what sites do *you* revisit and why?

You don't have to reinvent the wheel. You only have to read e-mail addressed to you. And you can and should visit website after website, each landing adding another bit of background to your analytical base. Some websites will grab you. Some will repel you. Some will leave you with an "I wonder why I'm here" feeling.

Start analyzing why you click out of an e-mail message after reading just half a dozen words. Start translating comparative advantages and disadvantages of various sites into your own planning. At worst, you'll reflect an approach you personally like. At best, what you like is what others also will like.

## What the Web Is and How It Can Work for You: A Two-Minute Primer

Simply put, the Web is the Mount Everest of information. Millions of computers worldwide connect to the Web, adding their special content to this information stockpile. The Web is the world's biggest and most accessible library.

But wait, you say. Isn't that the Internet and not just its much-maligned stepchild, the Web? I'm a marketer. I want to use the Internet for information and use the Web, its child, to sell.

Here's one comparison that favors marketers over academicians.

Certainly the Internet is bigger than the Web. It has to be, since the Web is just one component of the Internet. But how about saying the Internet is easy to access? Hardly.

First of all, most Internet addresses aren't commercial. Finding them is a chore in itself. Second, some require encryption information that you don't have unless you're an insider. Third, some Internet locations have become so paranoid (with good reason) about hackers cracking into sites to change academic grades, swipe government or industrial secrets, or transfer huge sums of money into their bank accounts that outsiders can struggle for months to gain access.

Not so the Web. The Web wants you. Some websites want you so desperately they run huge space ads in other media promising special rewards for abandoning those media in favor of Web visits (a questionable marketing tactic).

That, in fact, typifies the difference between the Internet as a whole and the Web as its own medium. But some sites are so vast, so endless, that even though you're where you want to be, you're at the outer edge of the target. It parallels someone saying to a visitor, "I have a friend in America. Look him up."

Want an experience that easily could last until the next year's models are produced? Visit the website of any major automobile manufacturer. You'll be *engulfed* with information—sometimes 25,000 to 100,000 pages.

The advantage is that you don't have to visit a dealer or even buy a stamp. You don't have to listen all the way through a sales pitch. *You, the surfer, are in command.* The disadvantage is that someone looking for specifics can go mad, lost in the far reaches of cyberspace, unable to get to information that might have resulted in a sale.

Score one for e-mail over websites. E-mail either kills with one blow or dies then and there. But it's always available.

## What the Web Isn't

OK, you choose. The Web is just like _____:
(Please choose all that apply.)

        A.  TV

        B.  Radio

        C.  Newspaper

        D.  Billboard

        E.  Telephone

        F.  Other

The most appropriate answer: *Yes* to all.

Existing media usually outperform the Web in their own backyard. Listening to a radio broadcast via a radio is better than radio via a website. Realizing where this nascent medium surpasses existing media is the key to focusing on what makes the Web unique. This also is the key to effective marketing. Let's add one qualifier: *Properly used*.

## Connecting

Television sets, like television stations, work well. When a television set fails to find a channel, something major is wrong: the set is broken or the station is not broadcasting. This is a most uncommon occurrence.

Reverse that principle for surfing. An intricate electronic symphony of computers, connections, and software must work in perfect harmony for the Web interface to happen. A weak link or malfunction in the computer, the connection, or the software makes the Web experience irritating, slow, or dysfunctional.

Why does this happen with such irritating frequency on the Web, when an equally complex interrelationship—telecasting a signal and receiving it on your TV set—can occur trouble-free time after time for years without a single interruption?

For starters, the Web's remote control doesn't work that well. Pointing and clicking with a TV remote is like horseshoes or hand grenades—close counts. Pointing and clicking with a mouse, or typing in the necessary commands, tolerates no mistakes. One erroneous digit, one period or tilde omitted, and the annoying "Site not found" message bangs onto the screen.

Another negative comparison: The TV remote changes channels instantly. The browser changes Web pages at the Internet's whim. The waiting time for a Web page ranges from seconds for a fast connection to a slim page, up to many minutes for a slow connection to a fat page. That's why we insist on fast download, especially for the home page.

## Obsolescence

Full motion video, stereoscopic music broadcasts, telephones, and teleconferencing are examples of applications racing to catch up with expectations. But that doesn't stop the next new product or version launch. And any attempt to freeze technological progress in a book is doomed—witness the number of books on computer or Internet subjects that now sit on closeout shelves, no more than two years after publication.

All twentieth-century computer-related products will be museum candidates by the year 2003. Imagine, in the year 2003, a primordial computer whose operating system is DOS 3.0, which ten years earlier was the most common system.

In hardware, the original IBM "AT" model had a 20-megabyte hard drive and a revolutionary 80286 Intel chip. What an advance for the year 1984! That machine couldn't even load a typical word processing program today.

Traditional software upgrades take years; Web software mutates over months. Netscape and Microsoft, for example, roar through browser versions, slugging it out for market share.

And that is the driving force—market share. Let's not limit the determinant of market share to those who make websites possible; let's (as we do in later chapters) remember that the whole purpose of competitive marketing is to achieve and *hold* increased market share.

## What It Can Be

What's exciting, in this confusing milieu, is what the Web does better than other media. Why? Two words: bulk choice.

A good state-of-the-art television connection has maybe 100 channels. The Web has millions of channels, and it's just getting started. The Web puts the user in control, allowing the user to dictate what she wants to see next.

Now, understand: That's assuming the user knows where to go. That's assuming the user has the time to study, sort, and select the destination. And that's assuming that when the user arrives, the site is there as promised. That's *our* job as marketers.

Communication may be one-to-one, one-to-many or many-to-many. E-mail should *always* be one-to-one. Town hall meetings or community picnics exemplify many-to-many communication. Face-to-face or telephone conversations are one-to-one communication. A parent talking to children, a speaker addressing an audience, and a television broadcast are one-to-many examples. The Web communicates in all three ways. Mining the Web's potential means taking advantage of each communicative strategy.

## Show Me the Money!

In the waning years of the twentieth century, sex became one of the Web's few profitable industries. Just as sex drives videocassette sales, sex-related websites drive an astonishing number of website revenue models. These electronic peep shows sell access to pornographic pictures and videos.

E-mail was and is a major "tout"—that is, a way of seizing an individual's attention and leading, or, preferably, *linking* to a website. Tens of thousands of such e-mails relate to sex.

Does this outrage you—not as a competitor for Web attention, but on a moral level? An opinion you may regard as objectionable, but one that applies to all media, is that outrage has never caused elimination. Witness drugs, handguns, or for that matter the original attempt to stifle demand, the doomed Nineteenth Amendment to the U.S. Constitution—prohibition.

What works is the combination of education and obsolescence, which can kill any concept instead of wounding it or transforming it into a martyr. As long as demand exists, a supply catering to that demand also will exist. The Web proves this every day, and the disappearance of once-popular websites also proves it.

Several other industries have well-known websites. Web surfers have regularly purchased wine from Virtual Vineyards, music CDs from CD Now, books from Amazon.com or Barnes and Noble, and even cars from Auto Byetel.

Through the shakeout period—certainly, through the end of the twentieth century—a great many other industries have been revealing an Achilles heel that surprises nobody: websites can lose money as well as make money. That's why website owners and managers lose sleep. The *Wall Street Journal* pointed out, after the wildly successful public stock offering of Amazon Books, that the company had never yet shown a profit.

And this money- and sleep-losing exercise may cast a negative cyber-shadow on the Web. Having no website at all is often better (from both a bottom-line perspective and a public relations perspective) than maintaining a poor, consistently unprofitable, seldom-visited website—not to mention the technical problems attending maintenance.

Score one more for e-mail: Cosmetics mean little. Word choice means much. And word choice costs nothing.

The Web is progress. The Web is the twenty-first century. The Web, love it or hate it, is the communications giant of tomorrow. The trick isn't to avoid it; the trick is to make it work for you.

## Everybody's Doing It

Millions of websites and so few good ones! What's wrong?

That's a naive question. What's wrong is that the number of websites far exceeds the number of webmasters and competent companies that can combine technical with sales know-how.

Poor websites pollute and overpopulate the World Wide Web. From elementary school projects to major universities and corporations, web-mania sings the deadly mantra: Any website is better than no website.

Like a vanity license plate, a Website address became the corporate status symbol of the 1990s. An April 1997 survey of Fortune 100 companies found 87 of them on the Web. Everybody is putting up Web pages, but the same companies use e-mail only *within* the corporate structure.

Students in middle school, high school, college, even postgraduate students all take courses at their local schools, quickly becoming Web page designers. Their output joins the conglomeration on the Internet. Who will see these silly pages? That question is irrelevant, because websites are fun and easy to create. How about the message of the site? Oh, that—well, wait until we've put our site together. Then we'll worry about words.

Adding to the confusion, salespeople are aggressively selling websites. Website pricing and design philosophies too often fail to focus on what a website could do best in favor of a bells and whistles approach focusing on form instead of substance.

Without form, substance is too dry to swallow. But form should never *replace* substance. As we see in many television commercials, excessive attention to form can drown the message in sugary syrup. "Great commercial. Now, what were they selling?"

## An Impossible Prediction

Predicting the evolution of the Web isn't just foolhardy; it's impossible. Alexander Graham Bell thought the phone would be perfect for listening to concerts. Thomas Edison envisioned a huge market for movie projectors, one for each person watching a film.

In a medium as technologically circumscribed as the Internet, why can't a knowledgeable observer predict what comes next? It's because the medium is still in a period of experimentation. Neither sites nor surfers have settled into any pattern allowing informed prediction to have any validity.

No question and no argument: The Web has the potential to offer information, entertainment, and a wide range of products and services as well as or better than other media. That potential already exists in tens of thousands of sites.

Most technically adept critics agree that the Web's technology and infrastructure still have a long way to go. Future features that will increase a Web page's complexity or decrease downloading time had better be fantastic, because surfers are loudly demanding greater visual and auditory appeal with faster downloading. Most successful websites are using simple technology that enables them to load quickly, and psychologically or visually masterful images that stop the surfer in his tracks.

But a final admonition before we abandon the comparison between the Web and the e-mail that feeds it and feeds on it: No one has ever found an effective substitute for the dynamic use of words.

# 4

# Cyberjargon

A WOMAN walks into an automobile dealership, intending to buy a new car. The salesperson—no, make that *clerk*—who shows her the cars operates in his linguistic territory, not hers, throwing around terms like "MacPherson struts" and "overhead cams." She walks out, unsold. She doesn't care about struts and cams. She cares about how the car looks and how she feels behind the steering wheel.

Any business has technical aspects and "in-terms." The world of computers, e-mail, and online services is loaded with technical terms—new ones pop up daily. The purpose of this book isn't to tell you how to program hypertext markup language (HTML) or java applets—it's how to market in cyberspace. But to level the playing field (especially since we have used some of these terms in the text by necessity), some sort of glossary is in order. The following definitions will serve as a handy resource for you as you seek to understand the native language of the online world.

### Advertising banner

A link to an advertiser's website. Small rectangular displays on a Web page, banners range in size from 120 to 500 *pixels* (picture elements) wide by 45 to 120 pixels high. (Note: Because screen sizes differ, dimensions are given in pixels, which are spatial units, instead of more conventional dimensions. On a 17-inch monitor, a typical banner will be about 1½ inches high and about 4 inches wide.) Websites sell advertising banner space on a cost-per-impression or cost-per-click basis.

### Backbones

The major electrical "pipes" used to carry information on the Internet. Ever bigger backbones are needed to keep up with the increasing number of Internet users and more powerful Internet applications. Fiber optic cable, less than 1 inch in diameter, is the backbone of choice. At the time of this writing, the top speed, OC 12, carries data at over 600 million baud. The typical modem's top speed over conventional telephone lines is 33,600 to 57,600 baud. (See *bandwidth* and *connection*.)

### Bandwidth

A term used for Internet data transmission, bandwidth is similar to horsepower in a car. Website owners and users constantly bemoan a lack of bandwidth. Website owners rev up bandwidth by trimming byte-laden graphics and animation and adding more powerful servers. Website users rev up their Internet connections with emerging technologies like faster modems and satellite, cable, telephone, and maybe even electrical connections to the Internet. (See *backbone* and *connection*.)

### Bit

The basic unit of computerized information, which may be either 0 or 1. (Don't worry about it. Your keyboard translates bits into readable units.) Internet users send and receive information in bits per second (bps). Connection speed to the Internet is often measured by how fast bits are transferred. (See *byte*.)

### Browser

Software that allows a person to receive information (sound, text, pictures, and animation) and then formats that information through the computer. The browser allows one to easily display Web pages and navigate the World Wide Web. (See *World Wide Web*.)

*Byte*

Eight bits make up a byte, the amount of information needed to describe a single alphabetic character. A kilobyte contains 1,000 alphabet characters, a megabyte contains 1 million, a gigabyte contains 1 billion, and so on. (See *bit*.)

*Clicking*

On a Web page, the mouse cursor changes from a pointer to a finger when it stops on a *hyperlink* (more commonly called a *link*). Once the cursor is over a link, clicking on the mouse's left button tells the browser to leave the existing Web page and move to the linked Web page. (See HTML and *link*.)

*Connection*

A general term for the quality of the Internet interface. A connection is the combination of computers, modems, backbones, Internet traffic, and other pieces of the puzzle that determine how quickly and easily one uses the Internet. (See *bandwidth* and *backbones*.)

*Crash*

Failure. Your computer may crash. Your server may crash. Occasionally the Internet's domain name system crashes. That means you're out of business until someone fixes whatever has crashed. (See *domain name system* [DNS].)

### Cyber
A commonly used prefix tacked onto nouns to give them an Internet twist. For example, *cybergeek* refers to a computer geek.

### Cyberspace
A catch-all term used to describe the Internet's territorial space, originating from William Gibson's science-fiction novel *Neuromancer*. Somewhat similar to airwaves for radio or television, cyberspace is an ephemeral yet global universe.

### Digerati
The technologically elite members of today's society who use the Internet on a daily basis both as a tool and as a toy.

### Domain name system (DNS)
The Internet's way of exchanging names for numbers. Just as a telephone company assigns numbers to individuals and businesses, the domain name system assigns mnemonic website names called uniform resource locators (URLs) to a numeric Internet protocol address. After all, names are easier to remember than numbers. Unlike the phone company, which lets everyone named Smith keep the name, domain names are often handed out first come, first served. And only one Smith is available. Each country makes its own policy. (See URL and *internet protocol address*.)

### Dot

A period. For example, saying verbally "Communicomp-dot-com" reflects a website whose address is "Communicomp.com" on the Web.

### E-literate

Someone familiar with and comfortable using e-mail.

### E-mail

The Internet's most common function. E-mail lets users send text messages and computer files to other Internet users. With the growth of intranets—electronic networks within an office or business organization—e-mail has become the communication method of choice, replacing typed memos. (Knoll Pharmaceutical Company of New Jersey estimates that its intranet, used by some 600 salespeople plus trainees, has the capability of saving the company $1 million a day.)

### FTP

File transfer protocol, an Internet function that lets users send and receive files among any computers connected to the Internet. The computer's physical location is irrelevant. FTP is routine between computers situated thousands of miles from each other.

### GIF

Graphic interchange format, one of two commonly used file formats for graphic images, makes it easy to transfer images between different computer systems. (See JPEG, the other common format.)

### *Home page*

The front door, or first page, of a website.

### Html

Hypertext markup language, the computer language that typifies the way Web pages appear and connect with other pages. By clicking on words or phrases for which these connections or links have been established, the user moves to a new page or site described in the highlighted section. Understanding this technique is vital to effective Internet page construction. (See *link* and *clicking*.)

### Http

Hypertext transfer protocol, the communications method for moving documents across the World Wide Web. Following this protocol ensures that any two computers connected to the Internet may communicate with each other, regardless of make or operating system.

### *Internet*

A network of computers connected to one another. From four computers in 1969, this network now contains many millions of interconnected computers in every nation.

### *Internet protocol address*

Also called IP address. Each computer connected to the Internet gets its own unique address. (See *domain name system* [DNS] and URL.)

*Internet service provider* (ISP)

Also called service provider. America Online, AT&T Worldnet, and CompuServe are three examples of these businesses that provide access to the Internet, or allow you to go online.

*Java*

A programming language created by Sun Microsystems that works well for the Internet. The java virtual machine (JVM), packaged with most late-model browsers, works as a universal translator for running programs on a Web page. Java lets page designers attach small programs to hypertext links to animate pages, retrieve information from databases, or otherwise automate an activity. Early java applications tended toward bandwidth-eating visual flashiness, but the trend is changing.

*J*PEG

Pronounced "jay peg," one of two widely used file formats for graphic images that make it easy to transfer images between different computer systems. (See GIF.)

**Link**

Also called hyperlink, a highlighted line on the Web page that, when clicked, will take you to another Web page or website. The text of a link can be both underlined and bold and may be in a different color. (See HTML.)

### Microsoft

The world's biggest software company, with a near monopoly in the critical software that makes computers run (operating system). But in the browser market, Netscape, not Microsoft, has been the dominant player. At this writing, Microsoft's browser, Internet Explorer, was continuing its heavily financed campaign aimed at eroding Netscape's share of the browser market.

### Modem

One of many ways to connect to the Internet. Via a telephone line, a modem transmits information at speeds typically ranging from 14,400 up to 57,600 baud.

### Mosaic

The original browser that set standards for Internet use. Mosaic's inventor, college student Marc Andreessen, introduced his innovative Web-navigating application in late 1993. Mosaic added graphics to the then text-only Web interface. In 1994, Andreessen helped form Netscape.

### Netizens

The citizens of cyberspace. Anyone using the Internet is a netizen.

### Netscape

People often call Netscape their browser, though Netscape is actually the name of the company that supplies browsers called Navigator and

Communicator. Netscape's browser has dominated the Web. Microsoft is its major competitor.

### Offline

Disconnected from the Internet. If you don't have a phone, you cannot telephone. If you are offline, you cannot use the Internet.

### Online

Connected to the Internet. The opposite of offline. You cannot send e-mail or surf the Web unless you are online.

### Search engine

A website specializing in searching other websites. These customized librarians send out electronic robots to catalog tens of millions of Web pages. Web surfers query the search engine's catalog for Web pages containing specific words or strings of words. In a matter of seconds (assuming a fast connection) the search engine returns a customized Web page listing the relevant websites. Results depend upon the searching criteria, ranging from zero to hundreds of thousands. Advertising banners support the cost of this free Web service. Popular search engines include HotBot, Lycos, Excite, AltaVista, Yahoo!, Dogpile, and WebCrawler.

### Searcher

Someone using the Web in a driven, focused manner. For the searcher, the Web is more of a tool than a toy. (See *surfer*.)

### Server

A computer or piece of software that is attached to a network that dishes out information. The word refers to both a computer and to the specialized instructions for the computer that houses Web pages. The instructions tell the computer to send Web pages a user has requested.

### Software

A set of computer instructions. For example, WordPerfect and Microsoft Word are word processing software programs. A computer is not a word processor unless it has a word processing software package.

### Surfer

Someone using the Web in a loose, unfocused manner. For the surfer, flitting idly from site to site, the Web is more for entertainment than education. (See *searcher*.)

### Surfing

Moving, often aimlessly, from one Web page to another. Surfing the Web is a spontaneous series of Web page hops for fun and entertainment. (See *surfer* and *searcher*.)

### Url

Uniform resource locator, or a website address. Each Web page has its own unique URL. Most Web addresses start with http://www followed by a dot and a second-level domain name, followed by a dot and a top-level domain name. Typical URLs:

- The *New York Times* is www.nytimes.com
- Florida State University is www.fsu.edu
- The White House is www.whitehouse.gov

Respectively, the second-level names are nytimes, fsu, and whitehouse, and the top-level or generic domain names are com, edu, and gov.

### Virtual

Simulated with software; close to, but not real. You can virtually visit places (CIA, the White House, or NASA, for example) with on-screen images that will make you feel like you are almost on the premises. The terms *virtual* and *cyberspace* are logical cousins.

### VRML

Virtual reality modeling language, a computer language that makes it possible to create three-dimensional models, transmit them across the World Wide Web, and let people interact with them through their browsers.

### Webmaster

The person in charge of managing a website.

### Web page

A single page on a website.

### Website

A collection of Web pages. Websites range in size from one Web page up to hundreds of thousands of Web pages. Some websites, such as search engines, can create Web pages—the Web surfer's search criteria return a newly born Web page with the customized search results.

### World Wide Web

The component of the Internet that allows for a multimedia (sound, text, pictures, animation) presentation of information through Web pages. By convention, this is an integral part of most Web addresses (URLs).

As you read these definitions, you may already have added others to them. Or you may have heard others, wondered what they meant, and forgotten them. Don't worry about it. What matters, for readers of this book, is the ability to use cyberspace to sell. And that ability doesn't depend on technical terminology.

# Cyberstarters

## Web Pages and E-mail: They Ain't Twins

Web pages and e-mail reach customers differently. With e-mail, it's straight-ahead point and fire, sending digital missives to one or 1 million e-literate netizens. With a website, it's build it, hype it, and hope for visitors.

E-mail goes to the customer. This makes it inherently aggressive. A website hopes the customer will come to it. This makes it necessarily seductive.

So if you're a cyberstarter, be sure that you point and fire your e-mail in the right direction and be equally sure that your website brings in more visitors. Boldness and bravery count in both disciplines.

## Cybersleuthing

As netizens evolve from using the Internet as a toy toward using it as a tool, they quickly grasp how to decipher e-mail and Web addresses. For starters, e-mail addresses include the @ symbol; Web addresses don't. Most Web addresses start with http://www. And there are no spaces in any Internet monikers, whether e-mail or Web. The alphanumeric characters before and after e-mail's @ or the Web's www are non-stop strings separated by dots (periods).

The Web address for America Online is "www.aol.com" (pronounced "w-w-w-dot-a-o-l-dot-com") and the e-mail address for a person named "Someone" using America Online would be "someone@aol.com" (pronounced "someone-at-a-o-l-dot-com"). The common denominator in both addresses, aol.com, is the domain name.

## Domain Names

Deciphering domain names is quick, easy, and well worth the effort. Domain names help classify websites and e-mail senders and receivers.

Notice, we said *help*. Domain names do not identify; they just tell you how the organization connects to the Internet.

The last half of America Online's domain name, aol.com, means that America Online registered the second-level domain name, aol, in the commercial top-level domain, .com. The .com domain has more second-level names registered than all other top-level names combined.

In mid-1997 the glut of Internet addresses prompted a move to vastly increase the number of domain names. This area has become fluid, parallel to telephone area codes expanding wildly as the proliferation of cellular phones and fax machines gobbled available phone numbers. The seven-digit system obviously limits the amount of available numbers to 9,999,999.

Some of the proposed new domains:

**.firm** for business firms

**.store** for businesses that advertise goods for sale

**.web** for organizations emphasizing activities related to the Web

**.arts** for sites dealing primarily with cultural and entertainment activities

**.rec** for sites dealing primarily with recreational and entertainment activities

**.info** for providers of information services

**.nom** for individuals

Other top-level domains include .edu, .gov, and .org. A domain name ending in .edu indicates that the sender, receiver, or website has something to do with an educational institution. Likewise, .gov identifies a United States governmental organization. The .org domain contains mostly not-for-profit organizations.

And each second-level domain name is unique. For example, the .com domain contains just one ibm.com, one apple.com, and one jones.com. Deciding who gets IBM seems obvious. But does Apple Records or Apple Computers get apple.com? First come, first served is the rule. (Forget the Jones competition. That gets tough.)

Additionally, two hundred diverse countries and territories register domain names. Country-level domains end in two letters, such as .ch for Switzerland, .ca for Canada and .au for Australia. SwissAir's domain name, for example, is swissair.ch.

Rules and regulations vary widely, subject to national legislation and restrictions. Some countries restrict domain name registration to their own citizens, while others welcome domain name immigrants worldwide for a fee.

The Kingdom of Tonga, for example, does a lively business registering names worldwide in Tonga's catchy .to domain. Second-level names already taken in Tonga include welcome.to, tokyo.to, sold.to, business.to, and hotsex.to.

You can see that website addresses parallel vanity phone numbers. First come, first served is the common procedure for registering second-level domain names and e-mail addresses; but with the availability and participation of countries like Tonga, plenty of good names are left. And no numerical limitation exists. A total of 9,999,999 not only isn't a limit, it already has been surpassed. There is no limit; the potential number of names is infinite.

## Who Are You?

Which e-mail address would you prefer—45.234.097@compuserve.com or boompapa@boompapa.com? Although an infinite choice of e-mail handles and domain names exists, individual domains exercise control. One reason for the quick popularity of America Online, when it appeared, was its ability to allow names rather than a series of numbers and letters, as an individual address.

Your Internet service provider (ISP) hands out e-mail addresses. The ISP plugs you into the Internet. As you shop ISPs, investigate their e-mail address options. A multitude of websites offer vanity e-mail addresses for your dollars and free e-mail addresses for your eyes. HotMail, for example, gives you free e-mail along with targeted advertising banners.

Regardless of the domain, each e-mail address is unique. America Online will only let one person use the "Someone" moniker followed by aol.com. Only one "Someone@aol.com" exists. And America Online has over 10 million members. AOL hands out these monikers on a first come, first served basis, with 10 million e-mail addresses already taken and no limit to possible variations.

If you really covet a name and can't get it on AOL, don't despair. There are other Internet service providers besides America Online and other domains besides .com. Explore your options and choose an e-mail address you think fits you and will result in business.

One option for finding a snappy e-mail handle is another lift from the toll-free vanity phone numbers. The number 4 can represent for, fore, and four. How about 2 for to, too, and two?

- glad2@

- 4estgump@

Several websites sell vanity e-mail addresses. Vanity e-mail has already-registered domain names such as cowboys.com, biker.com, sky-diver.com, fisherman.com, scubadiver.com, skater.com, emailat.com, bond-trader.com, and iamwoman.com. For under $100 per year, grouper@fisherman.com or risky@bond-trader.com could be yours. All mail sent to your vanity e-mail address is automatically forwarded to your regular (albeit boring) e-mail handle by your local Internet service provider.

Other sites such as Juno and HotMail give away e-mail addresses. Free e-mail is great, but "yourname@juno.com" carries a price. To doubters, the address broadcasts suspicions. Perhaps this person can't afford a real e-mail account. Why is he hiding behind a free account?

# Fire! Oops—
# Start with Ready and Aim

As Chapter 2 explained, e-mail is a powerful yet dangerous Internet tool. E-mail's simplicity is its own worst enemy. Spur-of-the-moment or emotional e-mails may miss the point or come back to haunt the sender. All too often the sender launches an e-mail without refining it into a carefully crafted message aimed at the targeted audience.

In addition to planning the message (covered in Chapter 7), a savvy e-mail marketer pays special attention to addressing the electronic envelope and presenting the communication. The digital choices are not choices among different stamps, paper sizes, colors, or paper weight, as they would be in conventional printed mailings. Still, e-mail's envelope, called a header, plays just as important a role in the success of your electronic marketing as does the envelope of a conventional mailing. Elements such as your e-mail address, correct recipient address, and subject heading improve the chances of getting the right party to open an e-mail instead of generating a quick "delete." Ignoring or quickly glossing over these components may mean that the intended receiver never opens your e-mail or that the absolutely wrong (read: "antagonistic") receiver opens your e-mail.

### Addressing the Electronic Envelope

A great e-mail feature, a major advantage for the marketer, is that this electronic envelope comes with the "From" address already filled out.

Most e-mail software automatically enters the default address on outgoing e-mail. Obviously, this address must be correct with no exceptions.

To verify your "From" address, send yourself an e-mail. Bingo! You'll find out quickly enough if the address worked or bounced. (The incorrect e-mail address yields a different type of incoming e-mail, an automatic response telling you that your e-mail bounced, or was undeliverable.) If your own message hasn't arrived in your e-mail inbox, you can bet others' messages aren't getting through either.

Sending e-mail to yourself shows how your e-mail appears to others. This is an easy method for testing e-mail presentation techniques such as signature files and text layout. Since not all e-mail software works alike, treat this glimpse of your e-mail as a rough guide rather than a master blueprint.

### Bouncy, Bouncy

Unlike replying to an e-mail, sending an original e-mail requires filling in the "To" address. Otherwise, where does the e-mail go? And filling in a complicated acronym followed by the @ symbol and another acronym is difficult. It only takes one mistyped character to start an e-mail singing a modern version of the Elvis Presley tune "Return to Sender."

This irritating version of the song manifests itself in the e-mail's inbox when an incoming e-mail informs the sender that the outgoing e-mail never reached its destination. Other problems could generate the same result: in addition to an incorrectly typed e-mail address, the receiver's ISP, an out-of-date address, and even gremlins attacking the Internet can bounce e-mail back to the sender.

America Online is far and away the biggest Internet service provider. Like so many other ISPs, AOL occasionally suffers minor but frustrating e-mail outages. (To the sender whose income is tied to e-mail delivery, it isn't so minor.) And as more and more users plug into the Internet, the infrastructure sometimes falters. These technical hiccups, though, rarely last more than a few hours.

Just like a telephone or fax wrong number or a piece of snail mail stamped "Return to Sender," bounced e-mail happens. The bounced e-mail's subject heading clearly states this with terms such as "Warning message," "Delivery report (failure)," or "Returned mail: User unknown."

This automatic reply simply informs you that the e-mail never arrived. You need to know why. Don't let the subject heading or the gobbledygook of text scare you. Open your bounced e-mail message and read it through. Not too far down in the text will be a dialogue explaining why the message never arrived. Hunting down bounced e-mail addresses ranges from easy to impossible. Regardless, you should react. Your e-mail didn't reach its destination.

### Where Are You Pointing That Thing?

Incorrectly filling out the "To" (the intended receiver's) address bites the sender. It also can bite the recipient, who may be waiting for the message. Paying attention to "To" will ensure that the bites are less frequent and less painful.

In addition to the "To" address, most e-mail software comes with two other address fields for outgoing mail, "CC" and "BCC." These extra fields save time and effort by sending a carbon copy ("CC") or blind carbon copy ("BCC") of the original e-mail to other recipients.

The blind copy shields the extra recipient's identity. This polite feature reduces indiscriminate sharing of private e-mail addresses. The carbon copy is exactly the same as a noted copy in a traditional letter. It explicitly notes others sent this same e-mail. CC works well for disseminating a notice to others included in the digital version of a document.

With replies, e-mail software automatically fills in the "To" and sometimes even the "CC" address. This simple, automatic step can be deadly, so take heed—check the "To" and "CC" addresses before sending! The sender may not be who you think it is. This mistake happens all too frequently with e-mail lists and with mail forwarding.

### E-mail Lists and Forwarding

E-mail from lists often comes with a return address going out to all list members. You think you are replying to some bozo about his recent posting on the marketing list, but your ill-advised yet lightning fast response lands not only in bozo's inbox but also in the inboxes of everyone on the marketing list! Now everyone on the list knows what you represent and, possibly damaging, who you are.

An excellent e-mail feature is forwarding. One click or keyboard command can automatically forward an incoming e-mail wherever you like. This handy way to pass along information has caveats. The main questions: Should the e-mail be forwarded? Would the original author approve?

Forwarded e-mail can trick netizens, especially the newbies, who might not figure out who sent the e-mail—the original author or the forwarder. E-illiterates read only the e-mail's message and see only the original author. But the e-mail's header, specifically the subject line, notes that this is a forwarded e-mail. And the e-mail's return address points to the original author, not the forwarder.

Answering an e-mail couldn't be easier. The e-mail addresses itself. But be sure to double-check that this handy-dandy feature points your e-mail in the right direction.

## Subject Heading

A correct e-mail address guarantees that an e-mail arrives at the correct cyberspace post office box. So what? Like snail mail, there is no guarantee that a successfully delivered message will ever be opened, let alone get itself read.

Chapter 6 provides select words and phrases for grabbing the reader's interest and enticing him to read the entire e-mail. An e-mail's subject heading, though, definitely will increase or decrease the chances that your e-literate target will even open your e-mail.

In an age of information overload compounded by lack of time, savvy e-literates perform an e-mail triage, discarding dubious e-mail at the click of a mouse. With increasing amounts of spam (unsolicited commercial e-mail) clogging up e-mail inboxes, users are increasingly jettisoning suspicious unopened e-mail. Similar to tossing unopened junk mail in the paper recycling bin, busy e-literates toss unread e-mail into their e-mail software's electronic trash can.

Don't ever forget this invariable rule when you're composing your brilliant e-mail message: *Your best targets are the same individuals who get the most e-mail.*

What's the significance of this rule? You see it, of course. Competition for attention (and for response) is hottest with the targets who are your hottest prospects.

Most e-mail software tells the recipient the e-mail's date, sender, and subject. The subject heading may be your only hook, or that extra incentive necessary to prompt the receiver to open your e-mail. Give it your best shot with a short (one or two to seven words) subject heading, avoiding *obvious* hype and suggesting personal importance and significance for your message.

## E-mail Tips

If you're adding extra bells and whistles to an e-mail's appearance, do it thoughtfully and judiciously. Tinkering with these add-ons costs time, and worse, the end result may broadcast the wrong impression.

Advanced e-mail software, for example, labels outgoing e-mail from unimportant to very important. Ridiculous. The sender rates his own e-mail. Give us a break!

Who in his right mind would send e-mail labeled "unimportant" except as an attention-getting device that can work only once and only on a few people?

If the message isn't important, don't send it. If you're not sure of the importance, don't send it. When in doubt, don't send it. E-literates are a skeptical crowd, suspicious of e-mail arriving from unknown sources. For them, e-mail labeled "very important" smells of spam.

A simple rule: *If you claim importance, prove it.*

Done effectively, signature files are well worth the effort. This handy feature serves as an optional footer for outgoing e-mail. Presentations range from informative and creative to overbearing and loud.

The better signature files include catchy artwork and fun quotations, marking the message with the sender's personality. At the opposite end of the spectrum, loud presentations include PLENTY OF CAPITAL LETTERS, VIRTUALLY SHOUTING OUT LOUD; ASCII artwork; and borders using characters such as !!!!!!!!!!!!!!!!!!!! or ++++++++++. (Suggestion: Don't use a string of asterisks: **********. These represent kisses.)

Most signature files include the sender's telephone and fax numbers and snail mail and e-mail addresses. Incorporating a website address into the signature file whispers that you are a savvy Internet user and directs the reader to your website. Showtime!

As a rule, the fewer lines in a signature file, the more effective and more readable it is. You know your market and the image you want to present. Obviously, though, a more graphic presentation is on your website.

## Hey! Here I Am!
## Won't Somebody Say Hello?

Websites can get mighty lonely. Despite the hype, most websites gather cyberdust on some computer's hard drive. Visitors have to look for a website, find it, and most crucially, find a reason for returning to that same website. Helping visitors find a website is by far the easiest of these steps.

Even though there are tens of millions of Web users, not even a fraction of these users can be expected to visit a website. Websites with thousands or more visitors per week are the exception. Lonely websites are the rule. You can give away free money and not attract even a few. Not everyone with a telephone calls an 800 number, and not everyone on the Web visits a website.

Surfers arrive at a website by typing in the address or following a link. Including the website's address in an e-mail's signature file, in addition to traditional printed material, tells the reader that this person or company takes the Web seriously: they have their own website, they are wired.

But who cares that *you* take the Web seriously? The three people a typical surfer cares about are me, myself, and I. So a question the website has to answer, and answer *fast*, is "What's in it for me?"

Helping someone find a website is the easy part. The first visit to a website quickly establishes, in the highly judgmental mind of the seeker, whether that website is wired or tired.

## What's Your Name?

Catchy or intuitive domain names help visitors remember website addresses the next time they log on: sexy.com, nuthouse.com, bargains.com. Although old-time noncommercial Internet community members object to the marketing implications associated with domain names, the image exists.

A website address is part of the marketing package. Treat it as such. Make the time to explore the various top-level and country-level domains in order to get the domain name you want. Take advantage of this opportunity.

Even with easy-to-remember Web addresses, correctly typing in the sequence of http://et al. is an arduous way to move from website to website. Clicking on a link is a quicker, easier, and more relaxed way to surf the Web, if a link exists. Example:

*For more of the same, click here.*

Most links, ad banners included, are built into a Web page. These "hard-coded" links come with a variety of options that affect every facet of the marketing mixture.

The most obvious factor is *cost*, expensive to free. Another is *targeting potential*, pinpoint to broadside. A third is *volume of impressions* the site where the link is displayed attracts, tens to tens of millions. And the fourth is *creative presentation*, simple to computerized magical special effects.

Experts may debate the value of a specific link, but no one, expert or theoretician, can attack the four separate criteria—cost, targeting potential, volume, and creative presentation. All agree that links work.

The simplest formula for the unsophisticated Web marketer is to actively seek links with free, targeted, and high volume tendencies. These links exist; search engines will show you the way. Creative presentation? That's up to you.

## In Search of Search Engines' Searches

Search engines create a second type of link, an ephemeral, on-the-fly set of links custom generated for each query. When the query is over, the Web page disappears.

Web surfers call up hard-working sites like AltaVista, Lycos, and Excite; these search engines dig through their proprietary Web indexes, each index containing tens of millions of Web pages. When the surfer enters a few keywords, the search engine rummages through its entire index in a matter of seconds, returning a list of relevant Web pages.

Search engines return (and list) anywhere from zero to hundreds of thousands of relevant Web pages. The results depend somewhat on the search engine but primarily on the keywords used. Very broad keywords result in too many hits and very focused keywords yield too few hits.

For example, typing "hotel" would bring hundreds of thousands of entries. Typing "Sheraton" would bring fewer than one percent of the generic total.

Search engines often rank the relevant sites by estimated percentage of relevance and accuracy. Although each search engine uses a different ranking method, the Web page's title, text, and keywords figure into the equation.

You can see the significance for the marketer. In your key area of business, if search engines are ranking you below 70 percent, reconstruct your home page title, text, and keywords to help your Web page move up in the rankings. Usually the search engine will list only the first 10 or 25 entries, with the user given the option to call up the next 10 or 25, then the next 10 or 25, and so on. Figure your chance of being noticed if yours is number 7,500 in the listings, or even number 75.

## Rising Above the Cybermilieu

Often, search engines include each Web page's first few lines of text. This text is "stripped" from the Web page, regardless of whether the text makes sense. Picture captions and other layout features hinder this special opportunity to yield more search engine clicks.

This gives the cybermarketer another clue for rising above the anonymous milieu. If possible, include a short, compelling Web page description, sprinkled with Cybergrabbers (see Chapter 6) and Cyberdetails (see Chapter 7) at the top of a Web page. This brief opening, compliments of the search engine, helps convince surfers that this page merits their click.

Protocol isn't absolute, except for the page's title. A Web page's description is optional, dependent upon the page's layout and any other presentation decisions. The Web page's title, though, is mandatory.

## The All-Important Title

Imagine a book without a title. Preposterous! Yet many Web page designers ignore the title. The title appears outside the Web page but inside the browser. What a perfect place for using some of the Cybergrabbers itemized in Chapter 6!

The title also shows up in the search engine results. If the page does not have a title, the search engine substitutes http:// followed by the Web page's Internet protocol address.

Clarity counts heavily. *Repeat: Clarity counts heavily.* So Web pages should have names as their titles, not numbers. And search engines often use titles as part of the search process. Web pages with relevant titles rank higher on the percentage listings.

Notice the word relevant. Some Web page designers believe that "sex" is the magic word for the Web. They feel the word has a universal appeal, so incorporating it into a Web page's title should drive hordes of visitors to a website.

OK, so it drives hordes of visitors to your site. So what? Who *are* these visitors? Will they buy what you're selling? (Yes, probably, if you're selling sex. No, if your ploy is transparent.)

But misleading the surfer carries more damaging baggage with it. Aside from the irritation factor for those who think they're getting what they aren't getting, you aren't attracting the people you really want. It's like putting a sign saying "Fresh Fish" on the front window of a stock brokerage company. Those who come in will be bewildered, then annoyed for having wasted their time; those you want will never find you.

## Key Words

"Sex" also has a way of showing up in a Web page's list of key words. These words are invisible to the Web surfer, but they're highly visible to the Web's search engines. Key words are an easy way to increase the chances that a search engine finds a Web page and bumps the page up on the search engine's ranked list of pages.

But keep the key words relevant. Surfers don't like being tricked. Any surfer who has ridden her electronic surfboard through the Web even once or twice has been alerted to the existence—no, the prevalence—of misleading key words. It's an easy trap for the cybermarketer to fall into, but the results are not positive.

Norwoods, a New Smyrna Beach, Florida, restaurant featuring seafood and wine, used the following key words as part of its Web page. The user never sees this string of terms, but the search engines sure do. These key words increase the chances that someone looking for fresh, blackened snapper and red wine will find Norwood's Web page.

```
<META NAME = "KeyWords" CONTENT = "wine,
restaurant, beverage, food, drink, sales, online, direct,
gourmet, Florida, beach, New Smyrna, red, white, dessert,
champagne, steak, seafood, fresh, blackened, charbroiled,
sautéed, grilled, filet, prime rib, fish, snapper, grouper,
lobster, shrimp, scallops">
```

## Words Are the Principal Weapons

Although the Web features animation, audio, video, and pictures, words still drive much of the Web's content and for the foreseeable future most of e-mail's content.

That's it for theory and philosophy. Time to put them into action. The next chapter is chock-full of winning terms for your e-mail subject heading, Web page openings, Web page titles, and Web page key words.

Turn the page and pick a few. Keep experimenting until your own results tell you you've hit the hot button.

# 6

# Wild and Whirling Words

## In the Beginning Was the Word

The chapter title (from Shakespeare's *Hamlet*) and the first subhead (from the Bible) emphasize a point every civilized person already knows: Words are our weapons if we're communicators. And in the vast reaches of cyberspace, with millions of competitors hurling words like an insane mélange of bowling balls flung at cosmic tenpins, far more of those lexical bowling balls are landing in the gutter than are connecting with a strike.

You know the primary rule of selling in cyberspace:
*Stop the surfer in his or her tracks.*

But this is easier said than done. This chapter is designed to help the cyberspace marketer throw strikes and knock over more surfers or at least hold them until they've been exposed to the intended message.

The purpose of the two lists in this chapter is singular: to stop everyone who sees your e-mail message in his or her tracks. So we're dealing with openings that should work, regardless of what's being sold or hawked or recommended or pleaded in text or banners.

These are yours to use. But please, use them judiciously. One will match your sales pitch better than any of the others. Which one is that? It's your call. Make it a bright one.

These are starter lists. They're lengthy but are only a fragment of what's available. Use these lists, but keep adding to them. When a specific word or phrase grabs you, makes you read on, or generates a receptive attitude, add it to the list of words or phrases. If you add just one a day, in a year you'll have another 365. And in three years? You'll have a lifetime supply!

## Words That Sell

As you evaluate these words, evaluate all variations—plurals, verbs, and nouns ("flash" suggests "flashiest" and "flashier"; "passionate" suggests "passion"; "want" suggests "wanted").

Try stringing some of them together; but don't go so far that the message becomes artificial, like a little kid showing off the words she knows.

We explain in the next chapter that some of these words aren't as polite as those you'll find in pre-cyberspace media. If they offend you, then don't use them. But remember that you're dealing in a unique medium, one that was born minutes ago, a child of today.

## Individual Words

| | |
|---|---|
| absolutely | big |
| action | blah |
| advantage | blast |
| amazing | blockbuster |
| attention | bonanza |
| awesome | bonus |
| bad | breakthrough |
| baloney | bull |
| bang | bulletin |
| battle | buster |
| bazooms | cash |
| benefit | chance |

chaos

cheap

complimentary

confidential

congratulations

control

cool

coolest

crap

crash

crazy

crock

damn

danger

daring

dead

delightful

devilish

dirty

discover

dynamite

easy

effective

electric

electronic

elite

erotic

exciting

exclusive

exotic

explodes

exposé

fast

feast

fire

first

flash

flop

| | |
|---|---|
| fool | hit |
| forever | Hollywood |
| free | horny |
| geek | hot |
| gigantic | huge |
| gold | hurry |
| goofy | idiot |
| gorgeous | imagine |
| grab | immediately |
| great | immoral |
| guaranteed | important |
| hate | incredible |
| hello | innocent |
| help | inside |
| hey | intimate |
| hi | introducing |
| hidden | killer |
| hilarious | kinky |
| historic | kiss |

| | |
|---|---|
| live | notice |
| look | now |
| love | nude |
| lover | nuts |
| lucky | OK |
| magic | oops |
| meet | opportunity |
| miracle | orgy |
| mistake | outrage |
| money | outrageous |
| moron | passionate |
| mysterious | personal |
| mystery | perverted |
| naked | phony |
| nasty | platinum |
| nerd | pleasure |
| new | popcorn |
| news | power |
| nonsense | powerful |

| | |
|---|---|
| preferred | sexy |
| priority | sizzling |
| private | shocking |
| question | slap |
| ravishing | slash |
| raw | smart |
| relief | smash |
| report | sophisticated |
| revealing | sos |
| ridiculous | special |
| ripe | spicy |
| rotten | start |
| run | stink |
| scared | stop |
| schlub | stupid |
| schmuck | sucker |
| screw | super |
| secret | surprise |
| sensual | surrender |

| | |
|---|---|
| surviving | want |
| sweepstakes | warning |
| terrific | weird |
| tongue | what |
| tremendous | wild |
| trick | win |
| tripe | winner |
| uh-oh | wizard |
| uh-huh | wow |
| uh-uh | yeah |
| unexpurgated | yep |
| unlimited | yes |
| urgent | yummy |
| virile | zero |
| voodoo | zzzzzz |

Note: Ending with an exclamation point is reasonably standard. Consider changing singulars to plurals or plurals to singulars, adjectives to nouns or verbs.

**Phrases**

A catastrophe is waiting to happen . . .

Advance notice

After Friday, forget it!

Am I wasting my time contacting you?

An offer you can't refuse

An open letter to . . .

Aren't you ready for . . .

Aren't you ready yet?

Are you a gambler?

Are you broad-minded?

Are you having problems with . . .

Are you hooked?

Are you interested in . . .

Are you in trouble?

Are you involved in this?

Are you missing all the fun?

Are you missing out?

Are you ready for this?

Are you ready to swap?

Are you single?

A secret is hidden here.

As seen on TV

At last!

Back at last!

Be glad you're here.

Be glad you waited.

Believe it nor not!

Big bucks for life!

Boy, will you be glad you stopped to look at this!

Brand new

Break the barrier

Buy direct!

By the time you've finished reading this you'll . . .

Can you answer this?

Can you really afford to . . .

Carry a big stick—this one!

Cash in on . . .

Check this out.

Choose your weapon.

Click here for . . .

Click here, get . . .

Click here, you fool!

Craziest offer ever!

Did we make a mistake?

Did you know this?

Direct offer

Don't be a schmuck.

Don't bother reading this unless . . .

Don't look at me like that.

Don't make the mistake I made.

Don't play games with me and I won't play games with you.

Don't you deserve . . .

Do you know how to . . .

Do you know who did . . .

Do you know who I am?

Eat what you want.

Elvis lives.

Everything you ever wanted to know about . . .

First announcement!

First time anywhere!

Flea market bargains

Follow this carefully

48 hours from now . . . (or Just 48 hours from now . . .)

Free samples

Free stuff

Get it direct from . . .

Get on the fast track.

Get paid for . . .

Get paid to . . .

Go ahead. Waste time.

Got two minutes?

Great news!

Guess what!

Hard core

Hello. My name is . . .

Help me out.

Here's a no-brainer moneymaker!

Here's an offer you can't refuse!

Here's your chance to . . .

Here we go!

Hi, baby!

Hi! I'm . . .

Hold it!

Holy smoke!

Hottest link you've ever seen

Hottest new . . .

How broad-minded are you?

How did they do that?

How I . . .

How long am I supposed to wait?

How to . . .

How would you answer this question?

How would you like to . . .

I don't want any money from you.

If I can show you . . .

If you knew you could . . .

If you've been looking for . . .

I hate to tell you this.

I have a fast $100 for you.

I have a job for you.

I have a problem.

I haven't heard from you for awhile.

I have to be out of my mind.

I hope this is what you wanted.

I'll bet you didn't know this.

I'll go to hell.

I'll tell you, flat out: I make a lot of money doing this.

I'm about to give up on you.

I'm betting you guessed right.

I'm betting you guessed wrong.

I'm crazy . . . and so are you.

I'm damned if I do and damned if I don't.

I'm giving this away.

I'm glad I found you.

I'm going to make your day.

I'm going to pay you . . .

I'm here for you.

I'm out of my mind.

I must be nuts.

I'm waiting for you.

I predict . . .

It's about time!

It's a hit!

It's the patriotic thing to do.

It's your turn to . . .

It works for me.

I've developed . . .

I've discovered this!

I've had it with . . .

I want you back.

I want you to . . .

I will pay you $2,500 per week.

Jump into . . .

Junk mail? Hell, no.

Just posted.

Kiss your old [whatever] goodbye.

Knock it off.

Last chance.

Let's make a bet.

Let's make a deal.

Let us send you . . .

Like this? Like that? You'll love . . .

Live! Right here!

Look at this

Look out!

Look what I have found for you.

Love and passion

Lucky me!

Lucky you!

Make me an offer.

Miss this and you'll miss out.

Need some dough?

Never again!

No b.s.

No fees!

Not to worry.

Now available

Now or never

Now you can . . .

Official survey

Oh my God!

Okay, so I'm crazy. So are you.

Okay, why have we gone to the expense of contacting you?

One minute. One buck. 60 minutes. 60 bucks.

On your feet, kiddo.

Opportunity knocks!

Our research indicates that this message will be of interest to you.

Pass this up at your own peril.

Please don't tell me you've heard this before.

Private report

Rake in . . .

Read this twice.

Ready. Set. Go!

Right now!

Say goodbye to . . .

Secret information

Secrets of . . .

Should I give up on you?

Shy? Don't be!

Skeptical? So was I.

Solid gold

Special report

State of the art

Still undecided?

Stop right here!

Stop! You're on television!

Survival tip

Take a chance.

Take a deep breath.

Take a good look.

Take it easy, will you?

Take this and shove it.

Thank you for your interest in . . .

The best just got better!

The coolest . . .

The hot bazaar of . . .

The joke's on you!

The price is right.

The real facts about . . .

The true story of . . .

The truth about . . .

The truth now: Do you . . .

They don't want you to know this.

They're onto you!

This is a one-time notice

This is a private message

This is awesome

This is not a spam.

This is perfectly legal.

This is the last time you'll hear from me.

This is the only time you'll see this message.

This is what we aren't:

This is your lucky day.

This really is free. No kidding.

This works!

This works every time.

Time out!

Time to get moving.

Time to get started.

Tired of . . .

Today only!

Today's special

Too busy? Too bad.

Turn your computer into a . . .

Ugly news

Under 18? Go someplace else.

Under 18? Keep moving.

Unidentified flying object!

Unless I hear from you before . . .

Wake up!

Want a . . .

Want to cash in on . . .

Want to see the world's . . .

War is declared!

Was I ever surprised

Way over the speed limit

We did it.

We goofed.

We have a list of . . .

We're going to pay you . . .

We're ready. Are you?

We've finally done it!

We've raised the bar.

What a mess!

What a revolting development!

What do I have to do to . . .

What is the matter with me?

What is the matter with you?

What's the difference between . . .

What's your opinion of . . .

What's your passion?

What's your poison?

What the hell!

What this isn't:

When you consider

Where have you been?

Who do you think you are?

Who says there's no free lunch?

Who wants to be safe?

Why am I doing this?

Why didn't you tell me . . .

Why we don't want to hear from you by e-mail.

Why would anyone . . .

X marks the spot.

You don't have to . . .

You don't need a credit card.

You have a problem.

You have got to check this out.

You need this.

You'll be sorry

You'll go ballistic

You'll hate yourself if . . .

You obviously know how to . . .

You owe it to yourself to . . .

You're about to . . .

You're going to hate this.

You're not going to believe this.

You're one of a handful

You're on the fast track, baby.

You're out of your mind.

You're the first

Your first step

Your last chance

You've been recommended

You want it? We've got it.

You won't see this on television.

You worry me.

Note: When possible, structure your message as an imperative. Dynamics are in order in cyberspace. But, as we hope you agree, exceptions are what lift one message above the milieu. If an imperative seems harsh and artificial, switch to a "good ol' boy" or quietly confident approach.

Experiment. No two offers or deals are the same. No two cybersurfers react in identical ways, though they do run on similar tracks. Analyze your own reactions. Better yet, start marketing and analyze your results.

For infinite variety, combine. For example, the opening "Who says . . ." can begin a thousand questions. "Please don't tell me . . ." can begin a thousand teasers.

Or change person: "How did they do that?" could be "How did I do that?"; "What is the matter with you?" could be "What is the matter with me?"

Variety is available without changing words. For example, you can EMPHASIZE a word just by putting it in all caps. Capital letters are universal, unlike italics or boldface, which may not translate from system to system.

Above all, two imperatives:

1. Keep adding to your list as power words and phrases occur to you.

2. Eliminate words and phrases as your experiences prove them to be ineffective for what you're selling. (But don't delete them altogether: They may work for your next offer.)

Always be aware of the wordsmith's command: *Words are our weapons. Let's not fire blanks.*

# 7

# A Few Easy Rules for Effective E-mail Selling

## Mission Impossible: Duplicating Print Ads in E-mail

A MID-1997 survey indicated that 68 percent of e-mail recipients either ignore or actually don't read their messages. What kind of warning is this for hundreds of millions of potential message senders clamoring for attention?

The effective salesperson tailors the pitch to the targeted individual. That's a truism.

But within that targeting, rules change depending on two factors that affect online marketing more than any medium yet. Those factors are:

1. The medium is geared for speed.
2. The medium is solidly one-on-one.

## Understanding the Two Crucial Factors

Nothing is leisurely about online communication. Whether in a chatroom, surfing at random, searching for a specific piece of information, or deciding to investigate an offer, the user has a forefinger poised above the mouse. Click! Gone.

So although the Web has many parallels with outdoor signs and classified advertising, patience isn't one of those parallels. The cardinal rule of Web marketing reigns supreme:

*Stop the surfer in his or her tracks.*

To transform this rule from interesting to useful requires that the marketer be able to imagine herself as the recipient of the message, not the sender. What does that elusive, skeptical, impatient surfer want to see on the screen?

Unlike other media, where the audience can actually resent the voice of a counterpart, online customers seem to welcome being solicited by someone who appears to be a contemporary. That's because of the one-on-one nature of e-mail.

The two factors, on analysis, give cyberspace a huge edge over the three other one-on-one marketing techniques—the telephone, the letter, and the in-person sales call. The difference is huge and profound: If I send you a letter, call you, or come to your office or home, I have initiated the attempt to form a relationship. If you land on my website, *you* have initiated the relationship.

And even if I send you e-mail, the relationship is immediately more personal than if I phone you or call on you, because I have approached you on common ground, in a shared environment. The contact is not only personal, but is expected to be personal.

## Me, Myself, and I

The list of phrases in the previous chapter includes many that are structured around the first-person singular pronouns me, myself, and I; and some structured around the first-person plural pronouns we, ourselves, and us.

Suggestion:

Whenever possible, use singular instead of plural. If you accept the concept that cyberspace communication is one-on-one, then you have to accept the concept that a message from me strikes home more powerfully than a message from us.

Rapport. That's a magical word in any type of force communication. In the e-mail universe it's more than magical; it's incomparable.

How can anyone compare the possibility of establishing plural rapport with the possibility of establishing singular rapport?

## The Two-Piece Suit

Another major difference between an e-mail sales message and conventional advertising—print, broadcast, direct mail, or even Web advertising—is that a mandatory component of messages in other media, completeness, may well be a liability in e-mail.

That's because of an attitudinal shift that occurs when an otherwise normal human being turns to screen and mouse. "I don't have time for somebody to spill his guts" is a standard reaction to an overlong e-mail message.

So, like other media, grabbing attention is the first job; but unlike other media, in e-mail grabbing attention can be the end as well as the means. Conventional advertising deserves nasty criticism if the message grabs attention and then says, "Thanks for your attention" without a call to action. E-mail does very well by grabbing attention and then making the call to action secondary.

E-mail has two siblings—links and downloads. Of course, telling the recipient, "Click here for . . ." or offering a download option will result in defections; but a higher percentage of those defections are chaff, not wheat, than in any other medium. And certainly, including a multi-paragraph download, or one with graphics, in the original component will result in the loss of many who otherwise would have taken that second step.

## Conviviality, Please!

The rules of cyberspace communication are reasonably consistent. Establishing rapport, on any level, mandates the suggestion and acceptance of a simple notion: you and I share a common whatever (goal, lifestyle, religion, work ethic, recreational choice, automobile, computer savvy, computer ignorance, and so on). The existence of this phenomenon implies that with exceptions, contractions are in order:

- I'm, not I am
- isn't, not is not
- aren't, not are not
- won't, not will not
- we'll, not we shall or we will (note exception to follow)
- can't, not cannot (same exception as "we'll")
- other related contractions affecting conviviality

There are two exceptions.

One is standard in force-communication—avoid contractions when you want heavy emphasis. For maximum power, you wouldn't say, "I won't let this happen," you'd say, "I will *not* let this happen." Similarly, you wouldn't say, "I can't let this happen," you'd say, "I can *not* let this happen." So for utmost emphasis, we revert to the uncontracted form.

Note the wording in the previous paragraph. It's ". . . you wouldn't *say*," not ". . . you wouldn't *write*." Verbalisms are implicit in the rapport-building mechanisms of e-mail.

The second exception is deliberate posturing in a patrician tone. Don't use contractions if your message is olympian, immediately identifies itself as coming from a source the recipient accepts as authoritative, or immediately identifies itself as highbrow. But without that qualifier—*immediately*—you could be regarded as an affected, outdated communicator whose haughtiness founders on the reefs of twenty-first–century egalitarianism.

## Is Rudeness In?

One of the individual words listed in the previous chapter is "crap." One of the phrases is "Take this and shove it." Bad form, isn't it?

Certainly it's bad form. But it's also evolutionary form. Do we like what's happening in many areas of communication? No. Do we recognize the societal changes words represent and the need to stay with those changes and those words or be left far behind? Yes.

You're in command. Use the language you want to use; but use it to match the experiential background and the attitude of your targets. In our world of force communication, a ton of dignity weighs less than an ounce of response.

## The Value of Questions

Asking a question is always safe. Many a speech has grabbed the attention of the audience by opening with a question. This is even more true if the question has the word "you" in it.

Questions automatically involve your audience and are automatically interactive. On days when you're composing e-mail messages and aren't feeling particularly bright and inventive, leaning on this old dependable won't ever let you collapse.

## Tips

The use of headlines can be dangerous. The professional communicator knows when a headline is in order; the amateur destroys a message by using a pronouncement that generates only apathy in the reader.

In an e-mail stack (a pod or grouping of a batch of e-mail messages sent by a reseller) headlines are in order because they separate the message from others within the pod. They clamor for attention like newly hatched birds in the nest, adding value to the words and phrases in the previous chapter.

Should you capitalize key words in headlines? Yes, if you want the headline recognized as a headline. No, if you're after instant rapport.

Within the text, capitalizing words is a safe method for gaining emphasis. A multiplicity of programs can kill italics or boldface, but capital letters survive all translations.

Don't use words that imply the worst of all four-letter words: *work*. Such terms as *earn* and *learn* and *strive* and *try* may convey a desirable ethic, but they aren't response generators. So our targets won't earn money, they'll make money. They won't learn how to, they'll discover how to. They won't strive, they'll be there. They won't try, they'll succeed.

Reinforce the concept with reinforcing words. They won't just make money, they'll make lots of money. They won't just discover how to, they'll easily discover how to. They won't just be there, they'll be ahead of the pack. They won't just succeed, they'll succeed the first time, guaranteed.

Don't suggest distant results. Residents of cyberspace live in the now. They want results now. They want action now. So promises tied to the future won't pull response nearly as well as promises tied to now.

If you tease or tantalize, give a partial solution. Don't let it hang. Bait. Entice. Suggest. Then, to make the bait, enticement, and suggestion truly tantalizing, give the online prospect a peek.

## Good or Bad?
## You Decide

Here are ten typical e-mail sales messages. We've lifted them word for word off the Web, changing only some typos and the name to protect the guilty. And we've ended the sender's address with [e-mail address] or [website address]. Would you have written them this way?

After reading each one, make your decision before moving on to the next paragraph, where you'll see our opinion. (If you disagree, that's your option. Not even an inexact science, e-mail isn't a science at all.)

*Example 1 (just the opening sentence)*

**Learn 5 Essentials to Good Customer Service.**

This is execrable. There's that deadly word "learn." Plus, it's an obvious headline, with capitalized words—a sign that this is a pronouncement and not a one-to-one message.

*Example 2*

**ONLINE MARKETING INSIDER Sings Like a Canary!!**

**Thinking of using the internet to make money?**

**YOU NEED THIS INFO –> [e-mail address]**

Confusing. What is it? The word "insider" is e-mail worthy; but the recipient is left wondering what this is all about. "Sings Like a Canary!!" means what? It's good imagery, *if* the recipient knows what the subject is. With other messages lined up waiting for evaluation, that wondering may never translate into action.

*Example 3*

**MILLIONS OF EMAIL ADDRESSES ON CD. Best prices! Choose 10, 20, or 30 MILLION email addresses! It took 6 months to make these lists—you can GET THEM NOW. For details and prices email [e-mail address] or visit [website address].**

Not bad. One questionable inclusion: "It took 6 months to make these lists." Some may regard this as an offer of a dated list.

*Example 4*

TERM LIFE INSURANCE QUOTES ON LINE

Over 184 companies searched for you—no sales pitches or high pressure sales tactics! Visit our web site for your free quote at [website address].

One problem here—the reader quickly interprets "searched" as a past-tense verb, meaning "Over 184 companies have looked for you." That isn't what the sender means. It should have been stated as "We search over 184 companies." Reinterpretation is deadly in e-mail. "No sales pitches or high pressure sales tactics" is good copy, capitalizing on a benefit of cyberspace. But inclusion of an example would help generate a move to the website the e-mail message promotes.

*Example 5*

Passion . . . Are you looking for a way to bring greater passion and intimacy into your relationship? Is emotional communication at a low? Then visit [website address] for passion rejuvenation and more. E-mail: [e-mail address].

"Passion" is a good starter word; "Hot passion" might have been stronger. "Emotional communication" is too intellectual a concept for this type of message. "Passion rejuvenation" loses it; why not "to get back that hot passion"?

*Example 6*

Let us send you a FREE $10 Phone Card and information on how you and your company can profit by giving these cards away!

E-mail your postal address to [website address]. Limit one phone
card per address.

No major problems. This is a typical teaser. Putting "free" in all-caps is logical, because on the screen this word seizes the eye.

### Example 7

"Network Marketing" you do it everyday, but you're not
getting paid for it, YET. We have a service people need
and want, "Digital Television." Profit by referring others
to the largest technological shift in history!
Voted by experts as the #1 homebased business in
the U.S. & Canada. [toll-free number]

Unclear. The message might have been more dynamic if "Network Marketing" followed "YET." The tease is incomplete: ". . . the largest technological shift in history!" tantalizes without paying off.

### Example 8

We Do Your Sales! You Don't Have To Talk To Anyone.
Receive weekly checks—$100/sale. Residuals to Infinity!
Company in 2ⁿᵈ year. One-time out of pocket—Lifetime of savings!
Call [toll-free number].

Too spartan. You do my sales in what? This heading unquestionably isn't the strongest approach to whatever they're selling. (What *is* the strongest approach? Impossible to guess, because we don't have any information.) In this instance, the caps/lowercase heading is a mistake. Capitalizing "infinity" is a more serious mistake.

*Example 9*

> $5000 Guaranteed Credit Limit* American Banks*
>
> Major Bank Credit Card* NO Credit Check* NO Credit Reporting*
>
> Guaranteed Unsecured Regardless of Credit History*
>
> Earn Referral Income When You Refer Others*
>
> Absolutely Everyone WILL Receive a Card*
>
> $18,000 per Month Possible* WANT TO KNOW MORE???
>
> E-mail any messages to: [website address]

An OK e-mail ad. It might have been more effective with an aggressive opening question such as "Who says you can't get a major bank credit card RIGHT THIS MINUTE?" The word "earn" isn't necessary when "pocket" or "rake in" are available. The staccato nature of this message matches short attention spans. And what about "Everyone WILL Receive a Card" instead of "You Positively WILL Receive a Card"? In this instance "everyone" validates the offer by adding other candidates.

*Example 10*

> ENTREPRENEURS WANTED . . . Proven home-based business that transforms lives and leads you to wealth. Not MLM or franchising. Join a team that's making a difference. 24 hour message. Call [toll-free number]

A total cliché. The genuine entrepreneur has seen a thousand ads exactly like this one. Here is another offer that could profit from conversion to a question. But nothing except complete replacement could save "Join a team that's making a difference."

# A Longer E-mail Pitch

The ancient adage "It takes as long as it takes" applies to e-mail selling as much as any other activity or description. Here is a typical e-mail pitch that showed up on the screen of America Online subscribers. Ask yourself these three questions about it:

1. Is the message clear?
2. Is it too short to convince, too long to sustain interest, or the right length?
3. Does it have the elements to hold the attention, interest, and desire of an apathetic online individual?

(Note: Every line was centered, just as the text appears here. Boldface and misspellings are preserved.)

Dear Internet Subscriber:

The Internet is a wonderful frontier for the exchange of information.
However, it would not exist unless someone, somewhere,
was making a profit!
Nowadays it seems like everyone is placing an ad for some service
or product on-line.
Like TV Commercials, these ads can often times seem annoying, however,
they generate **millions of dollars** of income for someone!

**Don't be foolish! Your computer is not just a fancy calculator
and mail box!**
Now more than ever, you come in contact with so many different people.
If you only had a product to offer, with the power of network marketing
behind you, one could generate a wonderful income!

SO here is that product in plain English:

*Sell a Lifetime Subscription to a Wholesale Dealer that will guarantee the
lowest price on nationally advertised products and services! **

Plus, as a bonus, every new member will receive:
* FREE Motorola Pager *
Long Distance rates @ 10 cents a min., 24 hours a day
* Discount Catalog with %50 off hundreds of products
* Grocery Certificate Program valued at $200

The price is a one time fee of $200.
(With all the benefits, the program does pay for itself!)
**Your commission is $100 for that sale!**
**In addition, everytime your new members recruit 2 prospects,**
**you will receive a $200 bonus.**
**That's $300 income for each new member you sponsor.**

**Sponsor and Maintain 15 Members and receive**
**a BONUS $500 Per month car Allowance**

**Sponsor and Maintain 30 Members and receive a BONUS $500 per**
**month car Allowance and a BONUS $1,000 Monthlv Mortgage**
**Allowance!!!**

The benefits are wonderful and not all of them are even mentioned here!
Imagine if you sold only 3 a week, one every other day.
You would receive a paycheck for $900 !!
All you have to do is get people or businesses to call a toll free number.
They will be connected to professional operators who will
close the membership sale for you.

*SO START NOW and respond to this E-Mail*
*with only a simple 'YES' and your name.*

*It's a no obligation request for some more info.*
*I will contact you within 24 hours and you'll be ready to go.*
**YOU CAN DO THIS !!!! People do everyday !!!**

*Become* **a member and be your own boss!**
**Claim your** *own* **stake in this** *life.*
**If there is any doubt at all, just e-mail me with a question.**
**No responce and you will automatically be removed from list.**
**Please don not send "remove" messages.**

*The listing of products, brand names and discounts will blow you away!!!!
You'll never want to pay retail again on anything from new cars to air fare!

Have you formed an opinion? Ours is that it says too little about what we're expected to do and what the actual "deal" is. The point is fuzzy.

The statement, "SO here is that product in plain English: Sell a Lifetime Subscription to a Wholesale Dealer that will guarantee the lowest price on nationally advertised products and services!*" is *not* plain English. Are we selling to wholesale dealers (something of a paradox)? Is the word "subscription" apt?

Examples will outsell puffery. The multiplicity of exclamation points doesn't help the image of someone selling to unknown prospects. A key selling argument—"You don't have to sell anything. That's our job and we do it for you"—isn't stated clearly.

And toward the end, the patience of the sender seems to have run out. Misspellings ("everyday," "responce," "don") and apparently random italics impede acceptance of this as an offer worthy of serious consideration.

On the positive side: Centering the lines helps prevent reader fatigue. Use of boldface helps achieve emphasis (although boldface is overused in this example). Enthusiasm is an obvious asset. Those who see the possibility of making money without a lot of work, in a simple-to-operate business, may well respond.

## The Benefit of E-Mail Marketing

The benefit of e-mail marketing is apparent when one analyzes a message such as this one: If it doesn't work, the marketer knows it within hours, or a few days at most. Restructuring doesn't require a battery of layout artists.

The biggest benefit, if you have the time and money to employ it, is to test two, three, or half a dozen competing messages. What an education the results will provide! Now it's your turn.

The most profitable suggestion we can make to any serious cyber-marketer is to use these samples as a starting point. Every day, pick one or two cyberads and analyze them. How might you have composed them? What substitutions, exclusions, or additions might you have made to add potency? As your analytical abilities expand, so will the power of your own e-mail messages.

# 8

# Banners

## Begging for
## a Simple Click

THE difference between banners and links isn't always apparent. A link says "Click here for . . ." or simply contains a few descriptive words; a banner says, "Click me, please!"

Commercially, a more profound difference exists. Search engines such as Netscape, Yahoo!, Lycos, Excite, and AltaVista charge for banners. So does America Online. You'll find banners on the home pages; but links for outsiders are few on home pages because home pages are, necessarily, self-serving (and income certainly is self-serving).

Here is the wording from a typical banner:

**101 Decorating Ideas**

101 ways to do it beautifully:

Everyone will adore the way you adorn!

What is the intention? To get clicked. A link would have said "101 Decorating Ideas" and only that, because a link exists (on the Web as well as on a necklace) as part of a chain. "101 decorating ideas" (lower case deliberate) might be one of a number of listings between "home decor" and "interior paints."

Here's another banner:

**Keep your man entranced and happy!**

Sexy goodies, sent in a plain envelope.

Click here or you'll miss out.

As a link, the listing for this same item might be "Erotic products" or "Sexual happiness—unusual products for your male lover." The banner, with or without graphic treatment, adds an imperative to the description.

Another banner:

**Classic Jazz Collection**

Almost too good to be true—Nat King Cole,

Sarah Vaughan, Tony Bennett,

Dexter Gordon, Billie Holliday,

Cassandra Wilson, Jackie Terrasson,

and a host of other great ones:

Grab these special collections while they last!

A weight-reduction plan has the following banner. Notice that the banner is provocative rather than informational:

**Lose Weight—Starting Today**
What does your future have in common with
Arnold Schwarzenegger, Sharon Stone,
and a sideshow at Ringling Brothers' Circus?
CLICK HERE . . . and find out what you can do about it!

Why isn't there a signature, a toll-free number, or an address? Because this is a banner, and banners aren't self-sustaining. They say "Click me, please!" And we know, in banners and in life, that details impede a quick decision.

## We Pay for Banners . . . So They'd Better Pay Off

Take a look at the Barnes and Noble page (Fig. 8.1). Are these links or banners? A simplistic answer is that those with only text are links and those with graphics are banners. A more accurate answer is that those making a simple announcement are links and those with an overtone of salesmanship are banners.

Fig. 8.2 defines the difference between banners and links more clearly. The rectangles at the top qualify as banners; the listings below are links. Fig. 8.3 is a collection of links and banners. (Because these all are internal, the line between links and banners becomes murky. Mini-messages with suggestions might be considered either.)

Figures 8.4 and 8.5 are banners that appeared on pages constructed by a company specializing in the creation of banners.

**Fig. 8.1**
This combination of banners and links might be regarded as links only, because all the references are to proprietary items within the company. Typically, banners might be text, text and pictures, or just pictures; links are text only.

**Fig. 8.2**
Banners appear at the bottom of this page; links are listed alphabetically in the center. A common deficiency of banners is their construction for an in-group; others may not know what their intention or content might be. A line of type validating the reason for "Click me, please" can help attract those who otherwise would not see any relevance to their own interests.

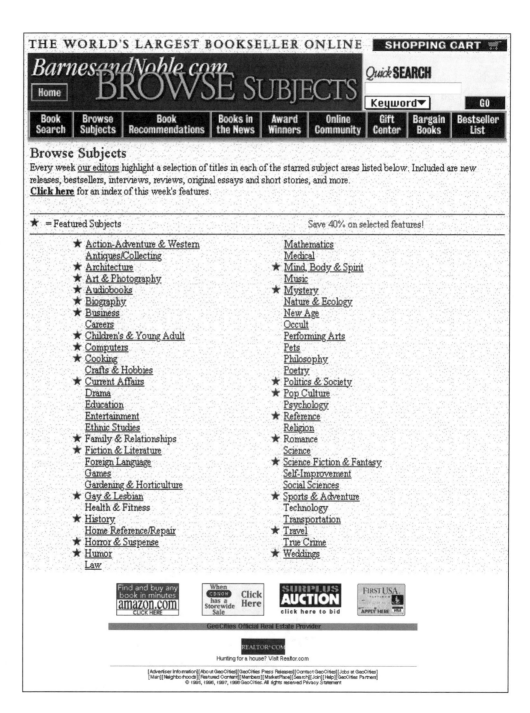

**Fig. 8.3**
This page is a combination of links and banners. Obviously, links are far more generic than specific; banners are product- or company-specific.

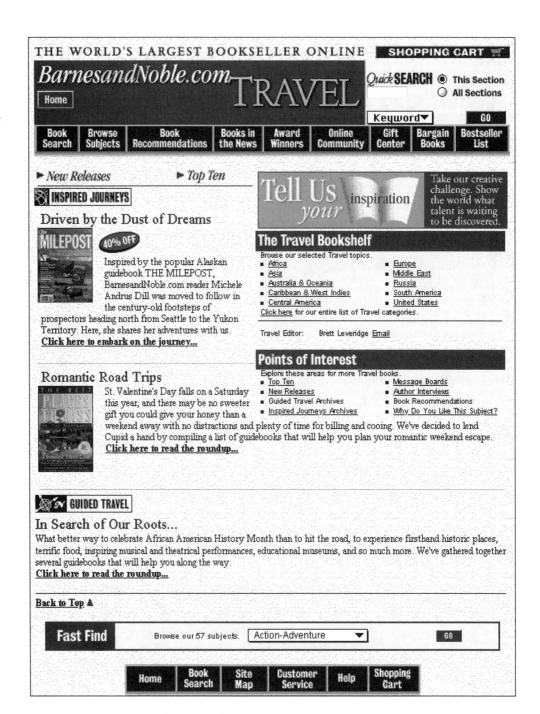

**Fig. 8.4 and 8.5**
Fig. 8.4 is an
exemplar of
samples intended
to sell others on
having this supplier
create banners for
them.

Fig. 8.5 is a home
page one
encounters when
clicking on one of
the banners or
links.

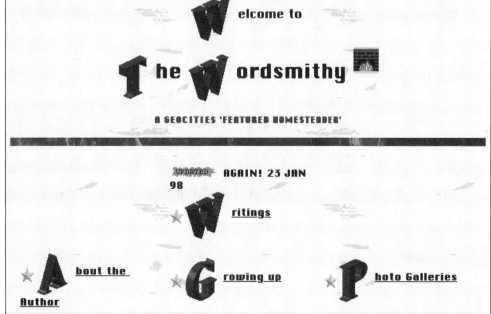

**Fig. 8.6**
A banner on Yahoo!'s home page (in this sample, the "Grammy webcast") will be seen by many. The major search engines usually rotate this prime position among their advertisers, allocating space on other pages for those who aren't featured here. Note the multiplicity of generic links.

**YAHOO!**
New  Cool                        Today's News  More Yahoos

'98 Winter Games                              Win an $8000
Tax Center    *visit the* GRAMMY®WEBCAST      Digital Theater

[ Search ] options

**Yahoo! Mail** - get your free @yahoo.com email address

Yellow Pages - People Search - Maps - Classifieds - Personals - Chat - Free Email
Shopping - My Yahoo! - News - Sports - Weather - Stock Quotes - more...

- **Arts and Humanities**
  Architecture, Photography, Literature...

- **Business and Economy [Xtra!]**
  Companies, Finance, Employment...

- **Computers and Internet [Xtra!]**
  Internet, WWW, Software, Multimedia...

- **Education**
  Universities, K-12, College Entrance...

- **Entertainment [Xtra!]**
  Cool Links, Movies, Music, Humor...

- **Government**
  Military, Politics [Xtra!], Law, Taxes...

- **Health [Xtra!]**
  Medicine, Drugs, Diseases, Fitness...

- **News and Media [Xtra!]**
  Current Events, Magazines, TV, Newspapers...

- **Recreation and Sports [Xtra!]**
  Sports, Games, Travel, Autos, Outdoors...

- **Reference**
  Libraries, Dictionaries, Phone Numbers...

- **Regional**
  Countries, Regions, U.S. States...

- **Science**
  CS, Biology, Astronomy, Engineering...

- **Social Science**
  Anthropology, Sociology, Economics...

- **Society and Culture**
  People, Environment, Religion...

What's New - Weekly Picks - Today's Web Events - Yahoo! Internet Life
Yahooligans! for Kids - Visa Shopping Guide - Yahoo! Style - 3D Stock Viewer

**World Yahoos** Australia & NZ - Canada - Denmark - France - Germany - Japan - Korea
Norway - SE Asia - Sweden - UK & Ireland
**Yahoo! Metros** Atlanta - Austin - Boston - Chicago - Dallas / Fort Worth - Los Angeles
**Get Local** Miami - Minneapolis / St. Paul - New York - S.F. Bay - Seattle - Wash D.C.

Smart Shopping with VISA

How to Suggest a Site - Company Info - Openings at Yahoo! - Contributors - Yahoo! How-To

Notice the banner (Fig. 8.6) on the home page of Yahoo!, a search engine. The banner is for ZDNet, the Ziff-Davis marketplace for computer products. Unlike links, which parallel classified or Yellow Pages advertising in that they may appear in a cluster of similar areas of interest or similar offers, the banner, when cast as a paid commercial advertisement, does not appear in the midst of a bunch of competitors. A banner on the home page of a search engine is the most expensive type of referral advertising on the World Wide Web.

## Negotiating for Banners

How much does a website charge for placing a banner on its home page? The question parallels "How much is a house?" in the sense that the answer is tied to traffic on that site.

Fig. 8.7 is an advertisement by an online mall offering banner space in the mall. At the time this was noted (late 1997), rates had been dropped from $150 per week for position in the mall directory to $100 per month. Another section offered a special—10 banners for $150 per month.

Was this a reaction to attracting fewer visitors than anticipated? Possibly. Might the lower rates have been the result of intense competition on the Web? Possibly. Could the lower rates have been a move to damage the ability of competitors to seduce advertisers away, or to attract advertisers? Possibly.

The conclusion many marketers reach, logically enough, is that rates are negotiable. Many home pages have "counters"—automatic electronic calculators that add one numeral each time a visitor lands. Unless the counter is attached to your banner, numbers tell only how many visitors *may* have seen your banner. Those numbers are not totally inconsequential; if your banner is visible and the visitor doesn't click on it, the fault can be with the appearance or wording of your banner, not with the location in which you've placed it.

## The Need for Analysis

Can a marketer exist profitably on the World Wide Web without banners? Certainly. No figures exist, but an educated guess is that fewer than 10 percent of Web marketers buy banners. The most common reason for not considering banners is that "They aren't noticed."

That may be. But those whose banners appear in prime locations such as the America Online home page or the home page of one of the major search engines point to definite results from these exposures.

One rule has to apply: Unless your banner says "Click me, please" and gives a valid reason for clicking, save your money.

## There Are Banners . . . and There Are BANNERS

Within the severe limitations of the medium, any banner has to either promote the company or promote a specific concept. Normally, we opt

**Fig. 8.7**
As the Web expands and the number of visitors expands with it, size alone will provide ample demographics for every interest and every taste. Online malls may be the clearinghouses of the future for banners and for the organizations placing those banners, just as shopping malls have supplanted downtown stores in urban areas. This mall advertises its current prices. Competition unquestionably will result in new malls arising and others disappearing.

Mallpark, Inc.

**ONLY**... Companies, institutions, agencies... selling goods, services or offering valued public services MAY LIST ON THIS SITE!

As the biggest mall group on the Internet, with 54 malls, more shopping centers and more merchants, we enjoy a TREMENDOUS foot traffic of shoppers.

It's a fact that free lists on the net are growing at a staggering rate and because so many are flooding the net daily it is easy to become lost in the huge and growing net crowd.... So Mallpark provides merchants a chance to upgrade...

and you don't have to be Donald Trump! $1.50 to $15 a month does it right.

Our best... is available at a GREAT price and... GOLD, SILVER or BRONZE Shopping Center Sites put YOU FIRST PAGE in all the right places with... our powerful search engine that only indexes keywords of this group. HIGH VISIBILITY FIRST PAGE EXPOSURE PRIORITY in SEARCH RESULTS Graphics, logos, more description available. Upgrade applications are subject to availability.

[ Upgrade to Gold, Silver or Bronze ]

**A reminder about the Free Tent sites...** They come with NO services and NO promotion.

YOU ALWAYS pop up in multiple pages BEHIND paying merchants. YOU get NO KEYWORD SEARCH capability AT ALL. IF your URL goes down, YOUR tent site is REMOVED without notice.

Before you decide to just be another "listing in the haystack"... We highly recommend you upgrade to at LEAST Bronze so YOU stand out and get keyword capability and FIRST page status. It's cheap enough. A year of Bronze costs the same as a night at the movies.

[ I just want a free Tent listing BEHIND the premium merchants. ]

Mallpark, Inc.
Email:mallpark@mallpark.com

© 1995, 1996, 1997 Mallpark, Inc. tm – Contents, Menu & Format U.S. & International Berne Convention for specifics to generate maximum clicks in this impatient medium. Take a look at the groups of banners in Fig. 8.8 and 8.9. Each is reproduced as it appeared on the World Wide Web—a solid page of banners. Would you have changed any? If so, to what, and with what result in mind?

Let's suppose you happen upon Fig. 8.8 accidentally (as we did, and as millions of others will, with the constant addition of new websites). Which of the banners on this page might grab your attention? Which might generate a click to get additional information?

Fig. 8.8*a* (Dining & Company) is category-specific but not product-specific. An example would help generate click-through.

Fig. 8.8*b* (The Ferret Store) differs from 8.8*a* in that the category itself is so specialized the banner doesn't require product teasers.

Fig. 8.8*c* (American Frame) is a simple announcement of existence. Would a statement of benefit, use, or special pricing have any effect in this non-competitive ambience? Most marketers would agree: It certainly wouldn't hurt. Even though the absence of competing banners is an obvious competitive edge, the surfer needs a spur—a reason to click on any banner.

Fig. 8.8*d* (The Vitamin Zone) states a competitive advantage—"discounted up to 50%." An example would undoubtedly increase the number of responses.

Fig. 8.8*e* (Sentimental Journeys, Inc.) neatly straddles the problem of being specific within a stringently limited space.

Fig. 8.9 is another page of banners. Fig. 8.9*a* (Hammacher Schlemmer) doesn't give a clue as to what this company has for sale. To prior

**Fig. 8.8**
Notice the heading on the page: "What's New." How many of these banners have any suggestion of newness? (None.)

## New Catalogs On Catalog Site

**Dining & Company**
Our collection offers exceptional items to make your kitchen beautiful.

Products designed perfectly for everyday living but elegant enough for entertaining.

**The Ferret Store**
The Ferret Store is your source for all your Ferret Supply needs. From food, to cages and everything in between!

**American Frame**
Custom Picture Frames. Customized

Services.

**The Vitamin Zone**
Over 5000 National Brand Vitamins, Supplements, Herbs & Minerals discounted up to 50%.
"Your new way to buy vitamins."

**Sentimental Journeys, INC.**
The most unique personalized gift items on the web. Personalized cartoon videos, audios, coloring books, and games.

customers of this catalog, the "teaser" is comprehensible; but failure to offer a single specific doesn't optimize the use of the space.

Fig. 8.9*b* (Interplanetary Pet Products) doesn't parallel The Ferret Store (Fig. 8.8*b*) in its lack of specifics, because pet supplies are far more generalized than ferret supplies.

Fig. 8.9*c* (Thunderbeam) does as much as it can with the space allocated. In this instance, naming a sample software title might actually *damage* response if the title doesn't represent a category the visitor might want.

Fig. 8.9*d* (Paula Young) deals with a specialized category. Like The Ferret Shop and Thunderbeam Software, categorization itself is ample reason for a click-through.

Fig. 8.9*e* (The Perfect Dress) is an excellent example of banner presentation. The banner gives those who happen upon this banner not only a statement of what is offered for sale but also suggestions for uses.

Figure 8.9*f* (One Hanes Place) has a hard-to-read logo—not ideal in the "seconds, not minutes" Web medium. The caps and lower case wording add to reading difficulty. But the well-known brand name unquestionably helps generate click-throughs.

The aggressive marketer has to keep two concepts in the forefront of her creative thinking: Specifics outpull generalizations; and the Web is not only the most competitive marketplace ever developed, but it will continue to become more and more competitive.

The simplest litmus test: Would *you* click on your banner if you were a casual passer-by?

**Fig. 8.9**
In the most competitive advertising medium ever devised, all banners are competitive with one another, because the online visitor has a finite amount of time. Once that visitor has clicked off the page, the possibility of returning to explore a competing offer is slight.

**Hammacher Schlemmer**
Offering the Best, the Only and the Unexpected for 150 Years.

**Interplanetary Pet Products**
Your source for unique and innovative pet products on the Web!

**Thunderbeam**
Thunderbeam: The smart way to shop for kids' software online, offering over 2,500 software titles and reviews, secure online ordering, and great prices!!

PAULA YOUNG
FASHION WIGS • 1-800-343-9695

**Paula Young**
Paula Young offers a wide variety of natural-looking wigs, wiglets, add-ons, and hairpieces for both men and women.

**The Perfect Dress**
An exquisite collection of special occasion apparel in regular and plus sizes. Perfect for prom, bridesmaids, mother-of-the-bride, cruises, and any other special occasion.

*The Perfect Dress*

onehanesplace  **One Hanes Place**
Famous Brands Of Hosiery, Intimates, Casual Wear & FitnessWear At Irresistible Savings.

| Index A-Z | Search | What's New | St. Patrick's Day | Gift Certs | Shop | View Order |
|---|---|---|---|---|---|---|
| Reviews | Newsletter | Dish | Sales | Gift Place | Magazines | CheckOut |

The Catalog Site Home Page